Working
with
Under 6s

VAL MULLALLY

Working with Under 6s

SCRIPTURE UNION

Scripture Union, 207–209 Queensway, Bletchley, MK2 2EB, England.

© Val Mullally 1997

First published 1997

ISBN 1 85999 180 7

British Library Cataloguing-in-Publication Data
A catalogue record for this book is available from the British Library.

Cover design by Mark Carpenter Design Consultants.
Illustrations by Dan Donovan.

Printed and bound in Great Britain by Cox & Wyman Ltd, Reading.

Contents

Introduction

Dr Luke's observations

Looking after children is a big responsibility, possibly one of the biggest many of us will undertake. You may, like me, have had both formal training in education and the experience of parenting. Perhaps you have trained but not parented, or parented but not trained. Or maybe you have no previous experience of working with children at all, and you picked up this book because you don't know quite where to begin!

Whether you are new to children's ministry or have already learned much 'on the job', whether you feel full of enthusiasm or in desperate need of refreshment, I hope this book will inform and encourage you. Above all, I hope it will help you see the 'big picture' and enable you to nurture the potential of the children you work with to grow into healthy, balanced adults.

One verse in St Luke's Gospel has been of great help to me: 'Jesus became wise, and he grew strong. God was pleased with him and so were the people' (Luke 2:52, *The Contemporary English Version*).

I read this verse many times before grasping its significance. Luke is, in fact, identifying the different aspects of human nature. It intrigues me that this statement, written nearly two thousand years ago, is completely in line with the latest thinking by educationalists. For an individual to be a whole, balanced personality, all aspects – the mental, physical, spiritual, social and emotional – must be developed. Jesus grew in wisdom (mental [cognitive] development); in body (physical development); gaining favour with God (spiritual development); and gaining favour with people (socio-emotional development which concerns interaction with other people: this is directly affected by emotional maturity).

In the next four chapters we will look at each of these aspects and explore how we can help the children we work with on their journey to responsible adulthood.

Chapter 1

'Jesus became wise'

A chicken hatches out of an egg and within a few hours can walk, communicate and feed itself. Humans are much more complex: it takes us eighteen odd years to learn self-sufficiency. This isn't just because of our physical development: our movements become more refined as we mature, but all the basic motor skills are achieved in the early years. For example, we may not be able to play a perfect game of netball at age six, but we can run and throw and catch a ball.

The fact is, as Luke observed, we are not just physical beings: we have social, emotional, spiritual and mental capabilities as well. In particular, our communication system is much more advanced than that of other creatures and we need time to develop complex skills. We need language to be able to share what we are thinking with one another, to express our feelings, to interact with others, and to have a relationship with God. Only when we have a firm grasp of language can we communicate effectively. This is the key to our human-ness. As adults, we often take our ability to communicate for granted. But when we work with young children – in whom the cognitive, emotional, social and spiritual aspects are still in the early stages of development – we may not be sure where to begin.

THE CHILD'S LIFE-WORLD EXPERIENCE

So you find yourself with a group of three-year-olds. They don't look like adults, they don't talk like adults, they don't think like adults. First, we need to realise that children are not 'mini-adults'. They have only been on this planet a few years and they don't have the experience and knowledge we have acquired. They are familiar only with their own homes and a small sector of the world surrounding their homes. They may visit the shop on the corner, they may remember their holiday at the seaside, but they only know what they have experienced. To young children, the next town, another country or outer space may all be equally beyond comprehension.

Every child comes from a different home environment, so we cannot assume that each will have the same knowledge and understanding, for this will depend on what he or she has experienced. I have always taught in an urban setting, but this year we moved to a rural area close to the famous Kruger National Park. This is an area where wildlife abounds. Many of the children are farmers' children, and I am intrigued by the totally different topics we sometimes chat about. A few weeks ago we were discussing what Daddy will have to do about the hippopotamus that's destroying the banana plantations! Only a child who has lived in this situation would be able to discuss such a subject. A city child would have no idea of a banana plantation, and if he has seen a hippo it would most probably have been in the zoo. What children know about, talk about and understand is directly related to their life-world experience. We must appreciate that their understanding and their language, both of which affect their thinking skills, are limited compared to an adult's. Consequently, young children have a totally different outlook to adults. Our challenge is to understand the child's understanding!

Understanding the young child

The little girl was standing on a downward slope when water started running from the gutter towards her. 'The water's chasing me!' she shrieked.

Children are naturally egocentric. They think that all people and situations are centred around them. From birth a baby opens his mouth in a wail and his parents are there to meet his needs. He thinks the whole world is there for his benefit. It is only as he matures that he begins to develop a broader understanding and realises that he is not the centre of existence. It would be no use trying to explain to that little girl about the law of gravity – she cannot yet think beyond her own immediate world, the one she has experienced.

Young children imagine that everything has a life and a mind of its own. Just as the little girl thought the water was 'chasing' her, so the child who hits his head on the table may turn around and smack 'the naughty table', not comprehending that the table is merely an inanimate object. We can help children realise that objects cannot deliberately hurt them by making comments that encourage them to see how their own actions may be responsible. So when a child bumps his head on the table, we can respond, 'You must be feeling angry that you're hurt. If you walk slowly, you won't knock into the table and bump your head.' But if *we* say, 'Naughty table!' the child will continue to view the object as the cause of his pain and not realise that the pain is, in fact, a natural consequence of his actions.

As the child's ability to think logically develops, we can help the process along by the example we set. When the children in my nursery class help me to clear up after a snack, I sometimes give Holly and Christo a small pile of plastic plates each to carry. I comment, 'We'll each carry a *small* pile, because if we try to carry too many we may drop them.' In this way I am encouraging them to realise that we can *plan* to do things properly so as to avoid accidents.

Seeing the world through the child's eyes

When your eye-level is at the height of everyone else's tummy button, it is only natural to have a different perspective. We need to see the world through children's eyes if we want to accompany them on their journey through life. This will involve retracing our steps and joining them where they are. We must match our pace to suit theirs, slow down, listen carefully and look at what they are looking at. Only the young child takes time to enjoy the wonder of a fragile butterfly, the persevering ant struggling with a load many times his weight, the insatiable caterpillar munching juicy holes in a leaf. And he has the curiosity and the courage to ask questions. He is trying to make sense of the world around him, how it works, how it all fits together.

Part of making sense of it all involves understanding days and weeks, months and years. Young children have no idea of chronological time. To tell them we will go to town in an hour, tomorrow afternoon or next week has little or no meaning. They are only aware of the rhythms of everyday life. This means that a regular routine is important to help them develop a concept of time and to give them a sense of security. A child cannot understand 'We will go to town at two o'clock or in ten minutes'. He can understand 'We will go to town after lunch'. Lunch time is something he knows, and if he has a regular routine he has some idea of how soon that will be. We can help children to develop a concept of time by referring to the regular routines in their daily lives, both at home and in the programme we run in our children's ministry. Young children enjoy the security of knowing that certain events follow one another in a certain order. They can understand 'We're going to have a story. Then we'll eat our snack. Then it will be time for Mummy to come'. When my husband goes away for a few days, years of nursery school teaching must have become ingrained because it's now only 'one more sleep' till Bill is home again!

Children also have little concept of time that has already passed. In their minds, 'a long time ago' applies equally to when Daddy was a little boy, when Jesus was on earth and when the world began! In fact, everything outside their immediate experience is 'a long time ago'. The advantage of this is that we don't need to tell Bible stories in chronological order. It won't matter to children if we move from Jesus to Noah to Moses. It's *all* a long time ago and they aren't concerned about what happened first.

DEVELOPING LANGUAGE

The child's experience of language

Young children have had only limited experience of language. They may not understand a word or may misconstrue its meaning. They may understand a word in a particular context and not realise that the same word can be used in a different way.

A minister friend was admiring the picture drawn by a pre-schooler learning about the infant Jesus. He asked the child to describe the picture. The child explained that Joseph was walking next to the donkey, and Mary and baby Jesus were riding on the donkey.

The minister noticed a large, black spot on the donkey.

'What's that?' he asked.

'That's the flea,' said the child.

'What flea?' asked the minister.

'Don't you know the story?' the child replied. 'The angel told Joseph, "Take Donkey, Mary and Baby and Flea to Egypt."'

This story may make us smile, but it's a good example of how a child's limited knowledge of language can cause misunderstanding. If children have only experienced a word in a particular context (as the word 'flea' in this illustration) they will try to give it that meaning. By using concrete objects and visual aids they can relate to, when we tell stories or chat about something, we make it easier for them to grasp what we are saying.

We need to use language young children can understand. As a child, I remember my father going up into the loft to fix the geyser. He expressed his concern that he might fall through the ceiling because the boards were very brittle. I remember my frustration in trying to understand what he meant. My father kept saying, 'Because the ceiling boards are *brittle*', but my difficulty was that I had an incomplete concept of the word 'brittle'. I knew it meant hard, and I couldn't understand why my father should be afraid that he might fall through *hard* boards. Wood was hard, metal was hard – they were hard and strong – so what was my father worried about? It was only when he used other words to explain the meaning of 'brittle' that I came to realise that it meant hard *and easily breakable*, like eggshells! My father repeating the same word didn't help me understand the concept: I needed him to provide me with other words I could relate to. I understood the word 'brittle' when I related it to 'hard', 'breaks easily', 'eggshells'. I knew those words, so I could attach meaning to an unfamiliar word. Try to use words that the children will know, and only introduce an unfamiliar word if you can link it to others that are already in their vocabulary. Speaking clearly and fairly slowly, using short sentences, will also help.

The value of questions

Young children are forever asking questions. 'Why?' must be one of the most common words in the pre-schooler's vocabulary! They are trying to understand their world.

'Why does the sun come up in the morning ?'

'Why does a millipede have so many legs?'

'Why do birds have feathers?'

These questions aren't silly. The child is trying to find out!

When children ask questions, we need to take seriously what they are asking and to respond simply and clearly. If you don't know the answer, say so. Show children that we can use books to find out about lots of things. Encourage them to think and to learn how to discover things for themselves. As far as possible, give them the opportunity to find answers through concrete experience. For example, if a child asks what happens to ice, let him experiment with ice and find out!

Ask questions in response to questions. Our natural response when a child asks something is to jump in with the answer. But if we respond, 'What do you think?', we will stimulate his thinking skills and mental development. Sometimes a child's observations can be very perceptive! So the next time you are asked 'Why does a spider have eight legs?', 'Why do bats hang upside down?' or 'Why did Jesus go in the boat?', try reciprocating with 'What do *you* think?'!

Accepting the child's viewpoint

We need to respond sensitively to children's answers. The little girl was too young to understand the law of gravity when the water 'chased' her down the slope, so to have told her that she was wrong would have been to discourage her from expressing her viewpoint. A better response would have been to receive her statement with a carefully phrased answer such as 'Yes, the water *is* running down the slope. It does look as though it's chasing you, doesn't it!' In this way, we are opening her mind to the possibility of another solution but not belittling her.

Recently I listened to a minister conducting a children's talk. He held up a fist-sized ball of green playdough, which he was going to use as an illustration for the story of Creation. He asked the children, 'What do you think this is?'

One little girl enthusiastically called out, 'A tennis ball!'

'No,' came the reply.

She hadn't given the answer he was looking for, but her answer *was* logical and her guess was as good a guess as any other – the dough certainly did look as though it might be a tennis ball. How was she to know what answer he wanted?!

A negative answer sends a negative message. None of us enjoys being told we are wrong, and we will soon stop volunteering answers if we think there is a chance we will be shown up. If a child responds with an incorrect answer, try to use a reply that won't deflate her. A better response would have been, 'It does look like a tennis ball, doesn't it? That was a good try. Can anyone think of what else it could be?' Then she would have felt good about her attempt at answering and brave enough to try again. Even if an answer is completely wrong, we can still thank a child for trying.

Asking questions encourages a child to think things through. It's easy to say something like 'Jesus went and had tea with Zacchaeus because he wanted to show him that he loved him'. But if instead we ask, 'Why do you think Jesus had tea with Zacchaeus?', we will stimulate the child's ability to reason and may gain some interesting insights into the way his mind works.

The skill of effective questioning

Learning how to ask questions is an important skill for the child carer. Different types of questions are needed for different situations. I alter my questioning technique depending on whether I am with a small group of children and there is time for relaxed interaction, or with a larger group where I need to hold everyone's attention. If I am in a small-group situation, I ask open-ended questions which encourage conversation.

'What did you do in the holidays?'

'Tell me about your favourite toy.'

'What are you going to do today?'

If I am having to keep the attention of a large group, or if I am in the middle of a story, I will be careful to ask closed questions that require simple, straightforward answers. For example, with the story of Jesus' entry into Jerusalem, I may ask about donkeys – an animal with which children in rural South Africa are familiar – to lead into the story. An unsuitable question would be 'What pets do you have?' This is open-ended and thus likely to distract the children from the story. Immediately, I have Molly holding the floor with details of Mopsy the bunny and Pluto the dog, while Johnny keeps butting in, wanting to tell me about his new kitten. Six others are waving their hands in the air, trying to get my attention, and the boys at the back have become bored and are pulling the hair of the girl in front. But a simple 'Does anyone have a pet donkey?' leads to a quick show of hands, and the story can continue without interruption.

Your choice of question will also depend on the children's life experience. If the setting were urban, it would be unlikely that any of the children would have a pet donkey. So I would ask 'Who has seen a donkey?' and try to have a good visual aid at hand to give the children some idea of what a donkey looks like. (Of course, a real donkey would be even better!)

Opportunities for developing language

With young children, try to work in very small groups – ideally not more than six and a leader – so that there are opportunities for informal chats while they are engaged in other activities. When you have presented your message or Bible story to everyone together, there may be an opportunity to chat afterwards with a few individuals while they are doing other things. But don't force your agenda. If children are deeply engrossed in drawing or making something, respect the fact that they are concentrating on that task. When we are working we don't appreciate distractions, and we need to offer them the same consideration. Leave it until you judge it is appropriate to have a conversation, just as you would with adults.

Be sensitive. What a child feels he needs to say is invariably far more important to him than what you want to talk about. He wants to be listened to carefully.

Encouraging correct language

When you are chatting with children, they will inevitably sometimes make grammatical errors. When this happens, respond by repeating the statement in question correctly as you continue your conversation. As always, be sensitive! If Jenny says, 'My mummy buyed me a new doll', it could be damaging to say, 'No, that's wrong. You must say, "My mummy *bought* me a new doll".' To correct her in front of all the other children may make her shy about expressing herself. A better response would be 'That's exciting. Mummy bought you a new doll! Are you going to bring her for us to see?' In this way Jenny receives the right language pattern but knows we are interested in her and her doll. Our response won't discourage her from trying to communicate.

Always avoid baby talk. Children will only have to learn to talk properly later on! I remember taking my toddler on a miniature train that chugged around an attractive park. As I gave him a running commentary on what we were seeing – 'Look at the ducks swimming on the pond!' – I became aware of another mother who was sitting behind me. 'Look – see birdie,' she cooed to her child. It can be tempting to talk this way, but if we resist we will naturally develop our children's vocabulary and teach them correct sentence construction. Young children learn new words by hearing them and relating them to their context. The more they hear a rich vocabulary properly expressed, the more easily they will develop a good command of language. This not only increases conceptual development as they learn what words mean, but helps them grow in confidence about being able to express themselves and make themselves understood.

The irony of this exposure to language is the spiralling effect that it has. Children with an inadequate command of language are likely to talk less and less as they sense their failure to communicate. The less they talk, the less they develop their command of language. Whereas children who are confident in expressing themselves will readily chat with others, including adults. The more they interact, the more language they hear and learn, and the more articulate they become. Encourage children to chat about things that are meaningful to them, and their language will develop naturally.

Children invariably understand far more than they can express, so provide a good language model, especially if a child is reticent about talking. In particular, be sensitive to any child in the group who speaks a different home language. You may make a wrong assessment of a child's ability if you judge this by language only. Children with another first language may have a good command of that language, and it would be unfair to evaluate them on the basis of their struggles to communicate in another. It's particularly important to provide 'hands-on' learning opportunities for such children – they cannot be expected to sit and listen if they don't understand.

The importance of understanding language

'Children do not construct meaning in a vacuum'.[1] When I was told that 'brittle' meant 'hard but easily breakable, like an eggshell', then I understood 'brittle' because I knew eggshells! A child can only grasp the meaning of a new word or concept if she can relate it to what she already knows. Every time we use a word it creates a picture or concept in our minds. The words we use represent concepts. Take a simple word like 'hard'. Think of something hard. Think of something not hard. When we use the word 'hard', we understand the concept of 'hardness'. We know that metal is hard, but cotton wool is not hard.

Words convey pictures to us so naturally that we tend to take this for granted. But young children have to learn every new word and understand the concept of that word. So a baby might be introduced to a dog and learn the word 'dog'. His parents say 'dog' to him every time he sees a dog or a picture of a dog. Soon he says 'dog' whenever he sees a dog. Gradually, he learns that there are dogs of all shapes and sizes – he learns the concept of 'dog'. Then he sees a cow. He has never seen a cow before. He says, 'Dog'. His mother responds, 'No, that's not a dog. That's a cow!'

The child presumes that this four-legged creature is a dog until he learns that it is a cow. When he learns 'cow', he actually improves his concept of 'dog' at the same time. A cow isn't a dog. As he has more experience with cows and dogs, he begins to develop a clearer concept of each. A cow is bigger than a dog. A cow doesn't live in the house. A cow eats grass and a dog doesn't eat grass. A cow moos and a dog barks. Through experience and language he comes to understanding.

A child has to learn the concept behind each new word he is introduced to. He learns those concepts by doing, by seeing, by touching and by hearing. He learns through interaction with the world around him.

LEARNING THROUGH ACTIVITY

God provided a wonderful way for young creatures to learn: we call it 'play'. We all enjoy watching a kitten stalk a leaf or chase a piece of wool. The kitten's play is actually its way of learning hunting skills and preparing for adult life.

Douglas Harbrecht writes: 'Many animals echo children's games. Monkeys play leap-frog, otters love king-of-the-hill, young hyenas engage in tug-of-war contests and young vampire bats play catch, chasing and slapping one another with their wings.'[2] Harbrecht notes that specialists in this field suggest that animals play hardest when their brain cells and nervous systems are developing the most rapidly. This research indicates that 'playfulness seems to be more deeply ingrained in animals with larger brains and longer maturational cycles. Thus whales and chimpanzees play more elaborately and for a longer time than hedgehogs or shrews.'

Play is how young creatures learn the life skills they need. Play is not a waste of time: to the young child, play is work!

Characteristics of play

Isenberg and Jolongo[3] outline the following characteristics:

*   Play is voluntary and intrinsically motivated. In play, children are free to choose the content and direction of their activity.

*   Play is symbolic and meaningful. It enables children to relate their past experiences to their present reality. By pretending to be others, they assume a 'what if' or 'as if' attitude. Young children often play house, developing their understanding of the different roles they see in their own homes. Six-year-old Nicole ends her imaginary telephone conversation to her 'husband' by saying sweetly, 'Bye, darling. See you later.' She is imagining herself in the role of wife as she has seen it modelled by her mother.

*   Play is active. In play, children explore, experiment, investigate and inquire about people, objects or events. Construction toys such as Lego give children the opportunity to create houses, cars, spaceships and countless other things. They are exploring, experimenting and investigating the potential of a toy. As they play, they are not only interacting with the play-objects but also with their friends as they create imaginative events together. The Lego car may be used to 'drive to work', or the spaceship will take them all on a trip to the moon.

    Construction toys are ideal play-equipment because they are open-ended: they can be constructed in multiple ways and for different purposes. This type of toy will hold a child's interest over a number of years as each new construction she tries presents a new challenge. Play is a learning, stimulating experience.

- Play is rule bound. Young children create and change rules during play that apply to appropriate role behaviour and the use of objects. We only need to think back to our own childhood games of hopscotch or cops-and-robbers to realise that children set their own rules.

- Play is pleasurable. In play, children pursue an activity for the sheer joy it brings and not for an external reward. We don't even have to ask them – they do it naturally. Our main responsibility is to create a stimulating environment that will encourage creative play. We must aim to provide one that is rich in learning opportunities that contain play-materials children will want to explore, experiment with, investigate and inquire about! This doesn't mean spending a fortune on equipment. Sand and water, wooden blocks and dressing-up clothes provide endless hours of meaningful entertainment for young children. We need only a few simple props to create an exciting environment for them to play and learn in.

The value of play

'Play enables children to create understandings of their world from their own experiences and exerts a strong influence on all aspects of their growth and development' (Isenberg and Jolongo). Play gives young children the opportunity to explore, to develop an understanding of their bodies and of their environment. They discover that they can run, jump and move in a hundred different ways. They learn how their bodies relate to the space around them. They observe how the world looks upside down, how sand feels slithering through fingers, how wet grass is slippery and concrete is hard. They learn how to use their hands and fingers to manipulate objects, and that there is a name for each object. They discover the properties of the materials they work with. They get to know about sand and water, about wheels and blocks, about pulling and pushing, about 'upside down' and 'high up on top of the jungle gym'.

We can never overestimate the value of learning through activity. Children need opportunities to solve problems and to develop language and conceptual skills. As they play with construction toys, they discover that blocks will stand only if fitted together in a certain way, and that different sized and shaped blocks can be used for different purposes. As they interact with each other and with us, they learn that words like 'longer', 'shorter', 'square' and 'rectangle' have particular meaning. It is through experience that children learn, and activity stimulates not only their mental capabilities but also their physical, social, emotional and spiritual development. Meaningful play needs time: a five-minute play-period means that children are only just settling down to 'doing their thing' when they are asked to stop.

As we come to understand the importance of play, we become less concerned about what the leader is doing and place more weight on what the children are doing. Although there is a definite place for activities such as storytelling, prayers and singing, we must acknowledge the tremendous value for children of prepared opportunities to learn through their own activities. We are there as guides to accompany them through an important part of their journey to adulthood. Our objective is that they learn through participation. To learn without active involvement would be like sitting in an armchair at home, paging through *National Geographic* magazines, rather than visiting those strange far-away places for ourselves. Real learning only takes place when we have 'been there' and used all our God-given senses to absorb the experience! As those responsible for children, our task is to provide rich opportunities for them to make discoveries, and to nurture their sense of wonder and respect for the world.

Notes

1   R G Gobbel, *The Bible: A Child's Playground*, SCM Press, 1986, p 63.

2   Douglas Harbrecht, 'Games animals play', *Reader's Digest*, August 1996, Readers Digest Association (Pty) Limited.

3   J Isenberg and M Jolongo, *Creative Expression and Play in Early Childhood Curriculum*, 1993, Merril/Macmillan Publishing Company (US).

Chapter 2

'He grew strong'

Once I was invited to observe the programme of the pre-school group of a large church. For the full hour they met, the children remained seated on benches, singing a few songs and listening to the leader pray and tell a story. After the session, her first question to me was 'Now, how do I get them to sit still?' I remember battling to answer diplomatically. Bubbling up inside me was the response, 'You don't! God didn't create children to sit still.'

Children naturally have a high energy level. They are constantly on the move. And they have a very short attention span. That's the way God made them. Our challenge is to provide a programme to meet their needs, not remould them to meet the needs of our programme.

PHYSICAL DEVELOPMENT

Young children are learning how their bodies work while they develop basic skills such as dressing themselves, using a paintbrush or a crayon, cutting with a pair of scissors or preparing a sandwich on their own. They enjoy these challenges. The young child's muscular control develops progressively from the head down and from the centre of the body outwards: so he learns first to control his large movements and only later gains fine-motor (small muscle) control. He learns how to use his arms, then his legs; control of his finger movements develops later still. So he may be able to throw and kick a ball, but he may not yet be able to cut with a pair of scissors. The younger the child, the more difficult he finds it to co-ordinate his movements.

Developing skills

Recently I attended a teachers' workshop on the significance of developing skills. We were put into pairs and had to stand shoulder to shoulder with our partner, facing a wall. The right-hand partner had to use her right-hand only and the left-hand partner her left-hand only, as each pair threw and caught a large soft ball. The activity caused much hilarity, but gave us a good perspective of just how difficult it is for young children to co-ordinate their movements. Throwing and catching a ball may seem easy to an adult but, like all skills, it is something that has to be learned for the young child.

Douglas Harbrecht defines animal play as comprising three basic components: mock chasing and fighting, repetition of locomotor skills, and a tendency of young animals to take dangerous risks. I have no difficulty thinking of examples of all three in children's play. Cops-and-robbers is a typical example of chasing. Ball and skipping games provide repeated practice of locomotor skills. And many of us will clearly remember climbing to the top of the tree even though our stomachs were churning in fear, just to prove we could do it! Through play, children develop their physical skills and, like wild animals, there are times when our very survival may be threatened if we haven't learned appropriate coping skills.

Each child's development rate is unique. Although researchers may speak of the 'average' child, there is no such thing. Often children aren't able to do the same tasks as their peers. Be sensitive to the developmental level of each child, and never try to push them beyond their capabilities. The child needs time for his bones, muscles and co-ordination to develop, and this is affected by his innate ability and experience. I once taught an intelligent boy whose parents were so involved in their careers that they had neglected their son's needs. Although he was well-fed and well-dressed, he had been given little stimulation, so at the age of six he had no idea how to hold a crayon or use a pair of scissors. He had never had the opportunity to develop these skills. Children need stimulation to develop their potential.

Each child is an individual: never compare one with another. Plan activities that will enable each child to feel satisfied with her achievements, and look for opportunities to give praise. Children thrive on encouragement.

PHYSICAL NEEDS

Our programme planning should centre around the physical needs of young children. Let's consider these one by one.

A safe environment

As those responsible for the safety of the children in our care, our first task should be to ensure that the environment we are operating in is secure, both in physical and emotional terms. Children are still clumsy at this stage and cannot adequately predict the consequences of their actions, so we need to be alert and to remove any possible dangers. This is discussed in greater detail in chapter five. We should also seek to make the environment safe emotionally, by instilling loving discipline and protecting children as far as we can from abuse. We will focus on these issues in chapters nine and ten.

A restful environment

A quiet, calm atmosphere helps children to settle down to tasks. Although it is normal for them to chat while they are working, encourage them to talk softly. Use of colour is important. Nursery schools often choose primary colours to create a cheerful look, but strong colours – especially red – should be used sparingly, if at all! Vibrant colours tend to cause hyperactivity, whereas pastels create a tranquil atmosphere. So aim to create an aesthetically pleasing effect.

It is also important to the children that their leaders look attractive! The same colour rules apply – very bright, busy fabrics are likely to cause over-busy children! Accessories, such as large gaudy earrings or jangling bracelets, can be a distraction.

Look good, but leave the bolder accessories for other occasions. Practical comfortable clothing is a must. Denims, track suits or long, wide skirts that give freedom of movement all work well. The leader's style of dress, gentle manner and quiet tone of voice all help to promote a restful environment.

Balance of activity and rest

Young children tend to have bursts of energy and then tire easily, so the programme needs to accommodate both active and restful times. Plan to have short time-blocks of leader-directed activities – that is storytelling, prayers, songs, and so on. However, the group will settle down far more easily and will concentrate better if you first provide a time of free play, so schedule in longer time-blocks where children can choose their own activities. They should be allowed to finish one thing and to start something new whenever they want to, and a choice of activities will enable them to decide whether they want to do something quiet or energetic. A few activities may be directly related to your theme for the day, while others such as block play and playdough can be 'regulars' and always available. For example, children can draw; or they can work off pent-up energy by twisting, bending, cutting or bashing playdough; or they can build with the blocks. It's widely recognised that we all need stress-relieving activities to ease the pressures of our hectic lifestyle. Children also have this need, and mistake-free materials prove to be excellent stress-relievers!

Time

Children need time to repeat activities they are trying to master. New skills need to be practised over and over again. This is why a simple task, like buttering a slice of toast, is so intriguing to children. They want to repeat the experience until they are confident they know how to do it. These tasks develop eye-hand co-ordination – training the eyes and hands to move in a synchronised way. As children master these skills, their power, co-ordination, speed and accuracy continue to improve. A child may, for example, be able to throw and catch a ball, but over the years she will learn to throw it further and more accurately, to catch it more easily and move more speedily. 'Practice makes perfect' is inborn in the young child!

Space

Children need space to move comfortably from one activity to another. If the playroom is cramped, they may lose motivation to try anything new. They need space to manoeuvre, to try out how their bodies move. If they haven't yet developed a sense of anticipation, they may run across the grass and bump into other children running in the opposite direction. Only with experience and enough room to move in do they learn to estimate such things as where and how fast to run and when to stop. Running, jumping, hopping and ball games are all activities in which children practise these skills.

Equipment

Children's skills are limited, so provide user-friendly equipment. Chairs and tables should be the correct height for little people. Imagine trying to work at a table that stands as high as your face! Paper size should be large (a minimum of A3 for the under-four-year-old). Drawing equipment, such as crayons and felt-tip pens, and brushes should be fat − about 1.5 cm thick − so that they can be held easily by little fingers. Paintbrushes should have short stubby handles. Children find long-handled brushes harder to balance as they work. Children under five don't have good enough fine-muscle control to work with slim implements or on smaller paper. To give yourself an idea of what it feels like for the young child to draw, put a very heavy glove on your wrong hand and try drawing with it! The younger the child, the larger the paper and implements should be!

Collect a wide variety of equipment to use in other activities such as baking, cognitive games, woodwork and practical life-skills. Children should be encouraged to work with this equipment so that they gain confidence and learn to use it safely. I love doing woodwork with young children. Often I am asked, 'Isn't it dangerous?' Yes, it is, but I take care when I buy equipment, and

I supervise the children closely. I teach them how to handle the tools correctly, and they know that if they disobey the rules I will immediately ask them to leave that activity. They love the challenge of 'real work' (even sand-papering blocks of wood is a satisfying tactile experience) and I have never had to do more than put a small plaster on a bleeding finger. Even if you don't have the equipment for a woodwork table, you may be able to borrow a few light, round-headed hammers for a special activity (don't use hammers with claws). Use fairly short nails with broad heads, so that the child has a larger target to hit. Have no more than six children in an activity group, and monitor them at all times.

Montessori schools have developed a programme of practical life-skills, where the children are taught to carry out tasks like polishing furniture, pouring water, fastening garments and sieving. These tasks are 'real work' in children's eyes and they thrive on learning how to carry them out competently by themselves. This type of activity can easily be done in the average group, because only ordinary household objects are needed. Try to find a Montessori school with a good reputation and arrange to be an observer for a morning.

Baking activities provide an opportunity to develop skills and to instil good nutritional habits. Of course, you will have to have access to an oven and the necessary kitchen equipment, and the food-preparation surfaces should be kept clean in line with hygiene regulations. If you meet in a church hall these facilities may be available, otherwise you could arrange to meet in someone's home. Encourage the children to prepare (and eat!) their own snacks. Spreading a piece of bread with butter is an achievement in itself for a three-year-old. Other simple tasks are peeling and slicing a banana, preparing fruit salad, grating carrots, making cheese on toast, peeling a boiled egg and making popcorn. Baking equipment can be improvised with plastic yoghurt pots and measuring spoons, and plastic cutlery is fairly inexpensive to buy. The best part of baking is that the children look forward to eating what they have made, and this is extremely satisfying for them in more ways than one!

Young children enjoy repeating activities, so choose things to do that are challenging enough for them not to lose interest but simple enough for them not to become discouraged. So, for example, if a new child in your group wishes to do a jigsaw puzzle, offer her a simple puzzle at first and observe how she copes with it. If she obviously has no difficulty, next time give her a more challenging one to try. But if she is struggling, encourage and help her when necessary. You could draw her attention to a part she is looking for, or discuss the picture the puzzle will eventually make, to help her understand where a piece may fit. Don't take over and do it for her, otherwise she won't have the satisfaction of achieving something herself. If she is given a fifty-piece puzzle at the start without checking on her ability, she might well become frustrated and lose confidence in trying to do a jigsaw again.

Plan to include in your programme several familiar activities and one that offers a new challenge. This gives children the opportunity to work at things they know and to enjoy the stimulation of doing something new. Too many new things at once can be overwhelming. If an activity is being ignored, it is likely to be too difficult, too easy or to have become overfamiliar. With activities like blocks and playdough, stimulate interest again by adding new props such as small plastic cars, dough-cutters, and so on. Evaluate the success of your activities by how much the children get involved in them.

A balanced diet and rest

Young children grow quickly, and need a balanced diet and opportunities to rest. None of us works effectively on an empty stomach, so ensure that children have had a balanced meal beforehand. If you are working in a deprived area, starting with a nutritious snack may be essential – even Jesus dealt with the practicality of hungry people (Matt 14:13–21)! If the children are with you for only a few hours, a sleep won't be necessary, but include both busy and quiet periods in your programme, to give them the opportunity to rest and relax. Follow up an energetic game with a quiet activity like storytelling, allowing the children to 'catch their breath'. Always have a 'cosy corner' with a mat and some cushions where they can be alone if they want to.

Support from an adult

The younger the children, the more they will need individual attention and therefore the fewer there should be in a group. The helper is a parent figure to them and must be readily available to meet their needs, whether this is showing them how to hold a paintbrush, tying a shoelace or accompanying them to the toilet. This age group hasn't yet developed many life-skills and is very dependent on the adult. With toddlers, there should ideally be one helper for every five children and less than fifteen children in each group. Two or more leaders working together with a younger age group have the advantage that if a child needs individual attention, the other leader(s) can look after group needs.

A choice of activities

Remember that very young children are confused by having too many choices. When working with the pre-schooler, a good rule is to have the same number of choices as the age of the child. So provide three choices for three-year-olds and five choices for five-year-olds, although a choice of six activities should be ample for older children. During activity time with a group of three-year-olds, you could have a playdough activity, a drawing activity and a cutting activity. With five-year-olds, I would include two more activities, such as collage work and painting.

If the group time is short – half an hour or so – and there is insufficient time for an initial period of free play, then a few well-chosen action songs and rhymes can be used as an 'energy burner'. Start with lively songs the children are familiar with, then move on to calmer songs or rhymes as you settle them in preparation for a short 'ring time' (when the children sit in a semi-circle and listen to the leader). It's well worth building up a resource file of the songs and rhymes the children enjoy.[1]

THE ROLE OF THE LEADER

Young children want to explore their world: they climb the rungs of the slide, and thrill at being up high and then speeding down the smooth metal surface. They try to find out about every new thing they encounter by using as many of their senses as possible. Only when the child is around the age of seven does sight become the dominant sense. As adults, we gain most of our information about the world through our eyes. But the first thing a young baby will do is put an object into his mouth or against his cheek. Very young children learn *kinaesthetically*, through the sense of touch. This is why a hands-on learning approach is so important in the early stages. Young children rely on multi-sensory experiences and learn more by doing than by sitting and listening or by looking at a picture. A picture is merely a two-dimensional symbol of a real object and has little meaning for the child unless he has already had direct experience of what it portrays.

In all aspects of your programme, make sure you involve the children. Activities like painting, playdough and drawing come quickly to mind (ideas on ways to vary these media are discussed in chapter eight). Outdoor play-equipment (eg hoops, soft balls) is another obvious way of encouraging children's physical development. But even during the ring time, when some leaders fall into the trap of 'taking over', children should be encouraged to participate. It may seem easier to do things ourselves, but children's direct involvement greatly increases the value of their learning experience.

Praying with young children

When praying with your group, it is helpful to use short phrases that children will understand. Many of us have childhood memories of simple bedtime prayers, like 'Gentle Jesus'. Children enjoy repetition. They learn by hearing the same words again and again: familiarity brings security. Saying a prayer where the children use a repeated phrase, such as 'Thank you for all the good things you give us, Jesus', usually works well. They also enjoy repeating each line of a prayer after the leader. But sometimes you may want to encourage them just to listen: this gives them a chance to hear how we can 'chat' to God. Pray about things they are interested in. Try to include their news within the prayer. A typical one might be:

> Dear Jesus, thank you that we can all come here today.
> Thank you for making Jonathan's granny better.
> Please make Russell better.
> Thank you for the lovely, sunny day today.
> Please keep us all safe. Amen.

Remember their short concentration span and try to keep prayers brief. The example you set will develop their awareness that we can talk to God anytime and anywhere. Sometimes I pray a quick prayer like 'Thank you, God, for this lovely, sunny day' right where we are standing in the garden. One of my strongest childhood memories is of my father kneeling beside his bed at night and praying. Actions talk louder than words. As a child I figured that if my big, strong daddy needed to pray every night, then I must need to as well!

Young children who have settled into a group often enjoy saying their own prayers aloud. Simple one-line 'thank you' prayers are a good starting point. I apply the 'same number of children as age' rule – if I'm leading three-year-olds, I choose three children to pray, and so on. Very often children tend to put their hands in front of their mouths and look downwards when they pray, ending up with an inaudible mumble. Encourage them to look up and to speak loudly and clearly so that the others can hear. Some children will be eager to pray aloud, but others may be more reticent. Using simple pictures of things they can relate to will help build confidence (eg a car, a woman, a man, a dog). Those who are going to pray choose one card each, stand and hold the picture, and say a short prayer. So a child might choose the picture of a car and pray, 'Thank you, God, for my daddy's new car.' The picture acts as a trigger for his thoughts.

Be creative and try doing something new. Go for a nature walk and pray about objects the children collect. Take a simple song like 'Thank you, Lord, for this fine day' and make up your own 'thank you' lines. Pass a ball of wool around, letting it unravel as it goes, and ask whoever is holding the ball to pray aloud if he wishes. After praying, that child throws the ball to someone else who can also have a turn. Look for imaginative ways of making prayer special to the children.[2]

Songs and rhymes

Choose songs that involve repetition – this will make them easier for children to learn – and only introduce one new one at a time. Some young children will simply sit and watch during singing time, but don't worry – they're absorbing by listening. Never force a child to participate. Instead, give an encouraging smile; he will join in when he wants to.

Simple percussion instruments are very popular. If you aren't able to buy quality instruments, the children could make their own. Two paper plates stapled together, with a few dried peas inside, make excellent shakers. With a bit of imagination, children can make all kinds of instruments to accompany their singing or for special effects in rhymes or stories. One important tip: teach the children a signal that means 'Stop' fairly early on! Practice it as a game, showing them that they have to stop playing immediately on seeing or hearing your 'Stop' signal. Percussion can become a deafening cacophony if it isn't controlled. Seat the children in groups, each group having the same instrument. For example, if you are doing a song where the children are divided into three groups, one group could have the bells, another group the shakers and the third can do the actions. After a few minutes, swap the groups around so that at the end every child will have had a chance to play something different.

Dramatisation is a great way of involving children in stories. At the egocentric age, they all want to be the 'star of the show', so try to make sure that every child participates. For instance, if in your story there are soldiers marching, let them all make a 'marching' noise by clapping their hands against their legs. Or they can make the noise of the wind and whip up big 'waves' with their arms when dramatising the story of Jesus and the storm. Again, make sure they know your signal for 'Stop'! Keep any instructions clear, involve the children as much as you can, and praise them generously for their efforts. It's not the perfection (or lack thereof) of the end product that matters but the pleasure of the experience itself. Children don't forget the things that are meaningful to them, and when they take an active part in the learning situation, it is meaningful![3]

Notes

1   For ideas, see Christine Wright, *Let's Praise and Pray*, Scripture Union, 1994; and Elizabeth Matterson, *This Little Puffin Finger Plays and Nursery Games*, Penguin Books, 1969 (reprint 1988).

2   See Judith Merrell, *One Hundred and One Ideas for Creative Prayers*, Scripture Union, 1995.

3   Further reading: Lindberg and Swedlow, *Young children – Exploring and Learning*, Allyn and Bacon (US), 1985.

Chapter 3

'God was pleased with him'

Some years ago my husband and I led a seaside camp for teenagers during the December holidays. This time of year is midsummer in South Africa, and we have a long vacation over the Christmas period. It is also the end of our academic year, and while we were at camp the senior campers received the news of their final exam results.

I noticed one of the girls, Miriam, sitting alone, staring out to sea. I thought she had probably received bad news, and I walked out onto the rocks to sit down beside her.

'I've passed,' she blurted out and began sobbing inconsolably. Over the next few days a trained counsellor and I spent time with Miriam. At first she was reticent, but as she began to trust us we were able to piece together the outline of her life. She had been so abused at home that school was her only security. She was upset because she had hoped to fail and remain in the only environment in which she had experienced some degree of protection.

We continued seeing Miriam for several months after the camp was over. The trained counsellor helped her work through many painful issues, and I became a mother figure, giving support and comfort when it was needed. Gradually, Miriam began to believe in her own ability, and found a job. It wasn't always easy. At times she would disappear for prolonged periods, and once we tracked her down in hospital. But she was becoming more confident that God *did* care for her and would help her build something beautiful and constructive out of her life.

41

Miriam's spiritual transformation directly affected her physical, emotional and social development. As she grew to believe in God as a loving, caring parent, she began to believe in her own potential.

Very few educational books make more than passing reference to children's spirituality. This may be owing to the fact that no human being can properly assess how someone is growing spiritually. But it is the most significant aspect of a child's development. As we gain an understanding of the many facets of the young child's nature, we will be able to plan a programme that will nurture his spiritual growth.

RELIGIOUS DEVELOPMENT

Miriam had difficulty recognising God as a loving parent because she had no experience of a loving relationship with her own parents. Children develop their spiritual understanding through the physical world they experience every day. Their concept of God develops from what they learn through other people. Faith is caught, not taught! If a child experiences love and acceptance she will believe in a loving, accepting God.

I once attended a Christian lecture where the key emphasis was a simple mathematical equation. The trainer scrawled across the full length of the blackboard:

$$\text{OUTPUT} = \text{INPUT} = \text{OUTPUT} = \text{INPUT} =$$
$$\text{OUTPUT} = \text{INPUT} = \text{OUTPUT} = \text{INPUT} =$$
$$\text{OUTPUT} = \ldots$$

She was emphasising the truth that we cannot give of ourselves unless we are receiving input into our own lives. This is true not only on a physical and emotional level, but also on a spiritual level. To be fired up for the Lord we need to be fuelled up! Regular worship and time for devotion are essential for our own spiritual well-being. If our goal is the spiritual nurture of children, we need disciplined time in prayer for each child in our care, for his or her family and for the other members of our ministry team. We cannot make an impact on children's spiritual development unless we ourselves are receiving spiritual nurture. Children's limited language makes them astute observers. It's not whether we speak about love and caring that matters so much as the example we set.

Concept of God

The language and conceptual development of young children limit their understanding of God. As their grasp of language improves and their experience of life broadens, so will their concept of God. They perceive that God is Almighty (he can do anything) and that he can intervene directly in our lives (a child will readily pray that God will take him to the birthday party that afternoon). Children view God as present and personal, the creator and the sustainer of life.

Concept of time and space

Since young children are naturally egocentric, anything that happened prior to their own personal experience is 'a long time ago' in their eyes. They cannot envisage a world different from the one they know. One youngster drew a picture of Mary and Joseph boarding an aeroplane. When he was asked about his picture, he explained that it was a picture of the flight to Egypt! Young children relate what they learn to their own life-world experience.

Concept of reality

Young children have difficulty distinguishing between reality and fantasy. This ability only begins to develop after the age of five. This will affect our choice of learning material and Bible stories. For example, a child under four cannot understand stories about miracles. Three- and four-year-olds enjoy simple stories that illustrate love and charity, such as Jesus blessing the children or eating a meal with his friends. This difference in the level of understanding between four- and six-year-olds is good reason to have two separate junior groups where possible. Even with five- and six-year-olds, it is important to emphasise that the stories in the Bible are true.

Children's limited understanding of the difference between reality and fantasy makes it hard for them to distinguish this difference even within their own thinking. A young child may say something that is untrue, and firmly believe what he says to be right. He isn't lying, he is only verbalising his fantasies. Endeavour to guide him into an understanding of reality without crushing his imagination. If a child tells you a wild and wonderful story, make a simple, noncommittal response such as 'That sounds exciting'. Don't scold him for lying – he doesn't intend to deliberately deceive or mislead. A young child was severely reprimanded by his mother for saying there was a tiger in the garden. She told him to pray to God and say sorry for lying. He came back shortly afterwards saying, 'God says that's okay. He thought that big cat was a tiger too!'[1]

Concrete thinking

Be sensitive to the child's level of comprehension. Someone once said in front of a little girl, 'I'm dying for a chocolate.' The child became very upset and wanted to know why the lady was dying! She interpreted what was said quite literally. We need to choose our words carefully when we are teaching something. Avoid phrases such as 'Give your heart to Jesus'. Young children don't understand symbolic language and may say that they can't take their hearts out, or worry that this means they will die. Check that children really understand the meaning of songs, and avoid those that use symbolic language and complicated, antiquated terms. Songs with words like 'Cast your burdens unto Jesus' have little or no meaning for children. But sometimes the old ones are the best! Consider the fundamental truth in the simplicity of 'Jesus loves me, this I know/For the Bible tells me so/Little ones to him belong/They are weak but He is strong'.

Careful choice of wording in a story is equally important. It is better to tell a story than to read it: by telling the story, you can use words you know the children will understand. Read the story several times to become familiar with it, and write down a few key words to help you remember the important points.

Then tell it in your own words. Stories presented in this manner come alive and capture children's imagination.

ACQUISITION OF LANGUAGE

As conceptual development is closely linked to the acquisition of language, a knowledge of the child's level of development enables us to respond appropriately.

Stages of language development

The three- to four-year-old

A child in this age group can use approximately 900 words. He is usually able to construct simple sentences, but unable to describe detail. He is beginning to ask questions about the nature of God, like 'Where is God? What does he look like?' If your answer doesn't satisfy him, he is happy to go on asking more questions. However, he may be content with the answer that God is in heaven and require no further explanation. When a child asks what God looks like, it is probably best to say that we aren't sure but Jesus is his Son and we can find out about Jesus in the Bible. Look at an illustrated New Testament together and chat about pictures of Jesus, but explain that this is what the person who drew the picture *thought* Jesus looked like. Perhaps you could ask the child to draw a picture of what he thinks God looks like!

This reminds me of the story of a little boy who was drawing when his mother asked him what he was doing.

'I'm drawing a picture of God,' he said.

'Nobody knows what God looks like,' his mother exclaimed.

'Well, they will when I'm finished!'

The four- to five-year-old

When a child reaches her fourth year, she has usually acquired a speaking vocabulary of approximately 1,500 words. She uses more complex and descriptive sentences, and gives human attributes to God, such as anger and fallibility. For example, she may perceive that God will be cross if she hits her baby brother, or she may be concerned that he will forget her birthday. Her relationship of trust with her parents and caregivers provides the foundation for an understanding of a God of love, truth, forgiveness and justice. She becomes familiar with these attributes as she sees them displayed in the significant adults in her life. She will probably ask numerous questions. At times it may seem that 'Why?' is the only word in her vocabulary! For example, she may ask, 'Why does the sun shine?' She doesn't want a scientific explanation, only a clear reason (ie to give us light and to make everything grow). She wants to know the purpose of things rather than the cause.

The six-year-old and over

By the age of six, the child will generally have a speaking vocabulary of between 2,000 and 2,500 words – more than double that of the three-year-old. She is able to use more complex sentences and expressions of time, such as 'yesterday' and 'tomorrow', though she still doesn't understand 'week' or 'month'. She becomes less egocentric and more interested in the surrounding world. She is more socially orientated, enjoys having friends and is able to converse with others. Her knowledge is broadening and she can discuss more topics. She inquires about God's actions: 'Does God sleep?' 'Can God see everything?'

Beyond six, a child will begin to ask questions about suffering and death. Typical are 'Where do people go when they die?' 'Why did Granny die?' 'Why do people get sick?' Children often ask questions that challenge us! I believe I have grown more in the understanding of my faith through ministering to children than through anything else. Even if we don't know the answers to these questions, our sincerity will count in the end. What children learn about Christian character through our example will be more important than giving them the right answer. It's better to be truthful and admit lack of knowledge than to concoct a story.

One child asked his mother, 'Where do I come from?' The mother took a deep breath and launched into a lecture on 'the

birds and the bees'. Finally, she asked him if he now understood. He replied, 'Yes, Mummy, but Kevin comes from London. Where do I come from?' Only answer the question!

Sometimes children's questions may seem like a veritable avalanche. Welcome them. They may provide a natural opportunity to chat about your faith!

SPIRITUAL AND MORAL DEVELOPMENT

Children are not born with an innate set of moral standards: they learn these from their parents and the people with whom they interact everyday. They are constantly observing how people behave and how they are treated, and this will affect their own emerging sense of morality. For example, if a child is brought up by parents who steal and who think that stealing is acceptable, he is likely to grow up believing the same. In a similar way, children learn about matters such as respect, fairness, consistency and concern for others.

Taking responsibility for actions

Children learn by the response they receive that certain types of behaviour are acceptable. They have an innate desire for security and feel unhappy when they face their parents' disapproval. They feel secure when they receive praise, and this is what encourages appropriate behaviour. As children's verbal skills increase, it becomes easier to reason with them, to help them perceive other people's viewpoints and to explain what the Bible tells us about how we should behave.

When five-year-old Raymond wants a toy, he tends to thump the child who has the desired object. Gradually, through careful guidance, he is learning that it upsets the other children when he hits them or grabs a toy away. He is now old enough to be able to discuss the situation. He wants to have friends, and becomes upset when other children refuse to play with him because of the way he has behaved. I ask him questions to help him realise that he makes the others unhappy when he reacts inappropriately.

'Raymond, why is Gretchen crying?'

'Did you have gentle hands?'

'What must you do now?'

'Can you ask her if you can share the toys?'

Raymond is beginning to respond in a socially acceptable way. He is learning that he must take turns and ask if he wants to play with something another child has. His interaction with his teacher and his peers is helping him to realise that bullying is not acceptable. This type of learning takes time. Occasionally Raymond reverts to impulsive behaviour. A child who is over-tired or unwell often resorts to less mature interactions.

At about the age of four, children begin to distinguish between right and wrong independently of their caregivers' approval or disapproval. They become aware of their responsibility for what they do, and experience guilt when they know their behaviour is inappropriate.

However, children don't have the reasoning powers of an adult. Consequently, they will judge right or wrong according to the damage that results rather than the intention of the perpetrator. Consider the following two situations outlined by Piaget. When John is called to the table, he accidentally knocks over a tray and breaks the fifteen cups it contains. When Henry reaches for the forbidden jam in a cupboard, he breaks one cup. Piaget's research indicated that children below the age of seven maintained that John was naughtier because he had broken a much greater number of cups (van Staden).

These points help us to realise that young children don't see matters of right and wrong in the same way as adults do. Our role is to guide them lovingly to an understanding of God's standards.

The young child's prayers

Children's spiritual development will affect their ability to understand aspects of prayer. As young children are egotistical, their prayers tend to be centred around the theme 'Please, God'. As they mature, they learn to say 'Thank you', but 'Sorry' prayers only become meaningful after the age of approximately six, when they begin to distinguish right from wrong and realise they are responsible for their behaviour. When we pray aloud on behalf of young children, we should endeavour to word our prayers appropriately for their level of development and understanding.

Unconditional love

I once counselled a mother who at times resorted to telling her two young sons that she was going to leave them if they were naughty. Comments like this cause painful insecurity. If a child has done something naughty, scold him, but don't undermine his confidence in your care and concern. Our unconditional love for children in our care will help them develop their own understanding of God's amazing unconditional love for us. One of the most incredible things about our Christian faith is that Christ died for us *while we were still sinners* (Rom 5:8). He didn't wait until we were perfect before he loved us – he accepted us as we are.

Building a positive faith

The days of preaching hell-fire and damnation are gone: it is recognised that people are drawn into God's kingdom far more by the realisation of his love for them than by fear.

Gavin was trying to cope with his parents' separation and was displaying mercurial swings in his behaviour. As an experienced teacher, I understood the emotional trauma he was going through and took as supportive a role as possible, even though he was naughty at times. One day he said to me, 'Mummy says I must be good. I mustn't let the devil get inside me.'

This child's negative behaviour was to be expected as he battled with the grief of a split home. Although I understood his mother's concern, putting the blame on the devil didn't encourage him to take responsibility for his own actions and may have contributed to his feeling of insecurity. As young children easily feel insecure or frightened, it is better to avoid talking about the devil or hell. Build their faith on the positive loving power and personality of our Lord Jesus Christ.

When laying the foundation of faith, be aware that young children are only just developing an understanding of right and wrong. They need our guidance to lead them to an understanding of God's standards. Use positive disciplinary methods which stress that we do right things because we love God, not because we fear punishment. Songs such as 'Be careful, little hands, what you do' can create an impression of God as a policeman who wants to punish us for anything we do wrong.

Trevor Hudson tells this story of Cardinal Basil Hume, Archbishop of Westminster:[2]

> He shared how he had been raised by a good but severe mother. Constantly she would say to him: 'If I see you, my son, stealing an apple from my pantry, I'll punish you.' Then she would add quickly, 'If you take an apple and I don't see you, Almighty God will see you and He will punish you.' It doesn't take much imagination to catch a glimpse of the harsh picture of God these words sketched in young Basil's mind! As his Christian experience matured, however, his picture of God gradually changed. Eventually he had come to realise, the cardinal testified, that God might have said to him: 'My son, why don't you take two?'

We have a generous, loving, holy God whose nature is revealed to us through Jesus Christ, a God who has freely given the 'apples' for our blessing and enjoyment! Let's nurture our children towards the realisation that God generously and graciously provides.

Notes

1   C van Staden, *Biblical Instruction*, Study Guide 1, University of South Africa, 1993, 1993.

2   Trevor Hudson, *Signposts to Spirituality*, Struik Christian Books (South Africa), 1995.

Chapter 4

'And so were the people'

I'm sitting at my computer, wrapped in a warm dressing-gown, with a box of tissues beside me. It is early evening and I'm recuperating from a bout of flu. Through the course of the day friends have popped in, bringing me practical gifts of lemons and groceries, a light-hearted cartoon book and, most especially, their love and good wishes. It's good to know that I have such caring friends.

Once the child's world expands beyond that of his immediate family, he begins to want friends. Children's social ability is not innate: they have to learn how to interact with others. A toddler may resort to tears or even pushing or hitting others in an attempt to persuade them to be his friends. We can help children learn social skills by providing an environment that gives them the opportunity to play, and we can guide them into acceptable social behaviour.

To build friendships children must learn to control their emotions. The more we understand their emotional responses, the more we will be able to provide a climate conducive to raising loving, caring, responsible people.

EMOTIONAL NEEDS

The parent

Parents are the child's first security. When children join the group, encourage parents to stay until they are settled, even if this takes a few days. (This is especially important if the group

53

meets only once a week. The infrequency of the group meeting will make it harder for a child to settle.) A new child is learning to trust a stranger. She will do this more readily if she has the security of someone present whom she knows. Parents will also feel more comfortable about leaving their children in your care if they have had the opportunity of seeing how you handle the group.

A younger sibling may want to be with her older brother or sister. Since establishing a trusting relationship is more important than the child being in the 'wrong' age group, let the older sibling stay with the younger child until she is settled.

A secure environment

Young children have come from the small world of home and may know very little beyond it. Stepping out into the 'big world' can be a frightening experience. They need a foundation of security and trust. They expect the same friendly leader to be there to greet them and look after them each week. They need the familiarity of the same room, of knowing where to find their favourite toys and seeing the same small group of faces. The group must be small enough not to be overwhelming. Children also like a regular routine and consistent expectations regarding their behaviour. For example, if they are not allowed to climb on the tables one day, then that rule should be applied all the time. They will be confused if rules keep changing.

Children's first experiences of church will leave an indelible impression. Even the youngest will have anxious, unhappy feelings about a place if they associate it with being left to cry unattended or in a soiled nappy, or to feel hungry or thirsty. Try to ensure that a child's earliest impressions of church are positive, happy ones. It is the leader who is mainly responsible for creating the right atmosphere.

Saying good-bye to the parent

The day will come when the parent decides it is time to depart. Encourage parents to actually say good-bye to their children: if they just 'disappear', they will leave their offspring feeling insecure. Children need to know that Mummy or Daddy is going now and will be back soon.

Parents should wait until children have settled down to an activity before they leave. Then they can say a word of farewell and make a swift departure. A child is more likely to be upset if her parent lingers. If it looks as though there will be problems, gently put your arm around the child's waist when the parent is preparing to leave. Close support of the child is reassuring for the parent. If Mary runs after her mother and clings desperately to her, it is upsetting for everyone and creates an 'out-of-control' atmosphere. Although Mary may not want me to hold her, she has the reassurance that I am in control and keeping her safe. If she becomes upset, I speak gently to her until she calms down, then I encourage her to join in an activity like playdough, drawing or playing with a construction toy. While the child is adjusting to the new environment, stay close by to offer reassurance until she has settled. Never leave an upset child to stand and cry by herself. Her crying is a plea for help and security. Always treat other children in the way you would like your own children to be treated.

If a child isn't settling into a group, be honest with her parents and encourage them to remain involved until she is able to cope without their support.

A foundation of trust

Try to set an example of kind, sincere behaviour. Trust is something that needs to be earned, and children will trust you if you prove trustworthy. They need to know that you are in control, that they can rely on your sympathetic support and that you are 'there' for them. We need to be astute readers of body language. The child who sits staring out of the window may need attention more desperately than the one vociferously demanding it right beside you. A teacher ought to have multiple pairs of eyes and hands – we seem so often to be needed in several places at once! It's not just about keeping an aggressive child under control: a sad child, or one who is quietly contented, also needs our attention.

Discourage children from bringing their own toys, as they are often unwilling to share personal belongings. The toy may not be robust enough to withstand the wear and tear inflicted by a group. However, allow individual children to bring any favourite dolls or teddies that function as a 'comfort blanket'. The familiar object will give a child a sense of security: let her keep it until she decides she wants to dispense with it.

THE LEADER'S EXAMPLE

Children are great observers and are quick to pick up any discrepancies in the behaviour of others.

I have always been a great lover of nature. When I was eight or nine, I belonged to a girls' club, and one day our leader took us on a nature ramble. We were each given a small box to collect something interesting along the way. I gleefully collected an interesting assortment of creepy-crawlies which are always in plentiful supply in Africa.

When we stopped for a lunch break, I proudly showed our leader the busy, wriggling contents of my box. Not comprehending the look of horror on her face, I left the box in her care while I rummaged around to find other interesting multi-legged fellows to add to my collection. When I came back a little later, I found to my consternation that my box, carefully left under a shady tree, had disappeared. The leader 'didn't know what had happened to it'.

I hunted and hunted, and eventually found the box. It had been thrown away with the struggling insects still sealed inside. They would have had no escape from their cardboard coffin baking in the hot sun if I hadn't rescued them. Suddenly I understood. I understood the leader's facial expression, why she 'didn't know' where my box was, that the nature walk wasn't really a nature walk, and that not all grown-ups could be taken at their word.

As we talk to children about Jesus, we must always be conscious that they will be looking to us to be the example of his sincerity, care and love.

Respecting each child as an individual

I love working with children, but I confess I don't find all children loveable. I believe that we are all naturally more attracted towards some personalities than others. Yet each child needs to know that he is special, so try to show equal affection and consideration to all those in your care. Their ability to 'read' body language quickly makes them aware of any discrepancies in an adult's behaviour towards different children. Treat them all with the same concern, and look for positive qualities to compliment in each.

This year I found it hard to like a particular child in the group, and it was obvious she was struggling in her efforts to make friends. Then one day I noticed what beautiful thick hair she had. I told her, in front of the group, how pretty her hair was looking that day. Her face lit up in a smile of disbelief. I really wondered if she had ever received a compliment before! She comes to me now with a beautiful wide smile, and somehow every time I see her she is becoming more attractive!

Encouraging positive behaviour

Each child is as unique in personality as in physical attributes. Some children are shy and retiring, others more boisterous. In the group I am teaching this year, I have three children who often respond with aggressive behaviour. For the past eight months I have tried to develop an ethos of 'kind hands' by setting an example and by discouraging all forms of violent behaviour. I encourage children to discuss any conflict situation they find themselves in and to tell each other how they are feeling. Two children have almost broken the tendency to respond aggressively, and the third child has greatly improved.

Physical health can be a vital factor in a child's behavioural problems. One particular child was prone to temper tantrums that at times disrupted the whole class. One day she was being downright impossible, and the other children in the group were becoming very upset with her. I realised it was going to be difficult to maintain the code of 'kind hands' I had been working so hard to establish within the group. When the children had gone home, I reflected on the situation. Was the girl's health the problem? We organised for her to see the clinic sister, and scabies was diagnosed. Suddenly her unreasonable behaviour made sense. The minute parasites had been causing her whole body to itch unbearably. No wonder she was acting like a bear with a sore head. Next day I explained to the other children that she had been cross because she was feeling so sick. When she returned, and the condition had been treated, she was a different child. Even after years of teaching experience, I realise I must never jump to conclusions. What happened that day was a lesson not only to me but to every child in the class!

Emotional health can also play a part in behavioural patterns. Children who are under stress at home may be difficult to handle. Thabo, who was well-behaved, has become excessively boisterous over the past few months as he tries to cope with his parents' divorce. I give him activities to help him work off his energy and anger, and encourage him to chat about his feelings, assuring him of my love and concern. However, I insist that the rules which maintain harmony in the group must be obeyed.

It's not always easy to be loving and caring when a child is acting negatively, but invariably he is the child who is most in need of attention. How he feels about himself and others will affect the way he behaves and learns. If we understand children's emotional responses, we are better able to know how to help them. A young child believes that the world revolves around him: his parents and others are there to meet his needs. He doesn't realise that the person who cares for him may also have other children wanting attention. It's only as children mature that they begin to understand that other people have needs and desires as well.

Children have to learn to share, but sharing doesn't come naturally. An only child won't have had the opportunity to learn how to share with others unless he is regularly interacting with other children. Children under three are too young to comprehend the concept at all.

Tara is playing with the large plastic truck. Kevin toddles towards her, his eyes keenly fixed on the attractive toy. The alert leader quickly attracts his attention: 'Look, Kevin. Wouldn't you like to play with this lovely new fire engine?' Kevin is happily diverted to another activity and confrontation is avoided. Try to provide an environment that will minimise conflict. Ensure there are enough interesting play-activities with which you can divert a child's attention, ideally *before* an upset arises.

TEACHING CHILDREN TO CO-OPERATE

Co-operation is a big lesson for young children to learn. They become upset when their needs aren't met. If Jamie wants the car Roald is playing with, he is likely to snatch it away or thump Roald. So I have to explain to Jamie that we aren't allowed to hurt other children, and encourage him to ask Roald to give him a turn with the car. Children must be encouraged to discuss and to resolve their problems.

Keep a delicate balance between reassuring children of your support, through your active presence, and helping them to learn to wait their turn and to co-operate. As they grow older, children become better able to communicate and negotiate.

Co-operation through play

The toddler usually plays alone. Up to the age of approximately three he may play alongside other children (we term this 'parallel play'). As he grows older he begins to interact more, and generally chooses two or three children as playmates. These are loose attachments and the child will frequently change his friends. He is equally comfortable playing with boys or girls until about the age of five.

Harbrecht suggests that through play, a young animal learns 'elaborate functions of social bonding and establishing rules'. He describes an incident when a young seal bumped into an adult and was bitten: 'The animals seemed to be learning what they could and couldn't get away with'. I smiled when I read that line – it's so true of children! Children 'test the water' in play and learn what is acceptable and what isn't.

Often adults try to impose their own thoughts and ideas on children. The following questions may test whether or not we are leaving them free to play. Is the child in charge of the situation? Are a variety of choices available? Is the child involved for the sake of the experience (or the pleasure)? Can the child pretend freely? Can the child freely engage in creative expression and behaviour?

True play leaves the child in control of the situation, and helps her develop understanding of social and cultural interaction. Provide an environment that is conducive to play, with telephones and dolls, dressing-up clothes (for boys as well as girls), simple props and construction toys. As children try out different roles, they will develop an awareness of themselves and of others. Through play they gradually begin to realise that others have different thoughts and opinions from their own. They learn to listen as well as to express themselves. They learn to channel their reactions into socially acceptable behaviour.

Yesterday, a group of boys were playing an imaginative game in the playground. 'You're the baby,' declared the leader to the youngest child in the group.

'No,' asserted the little boy. 'I'm the brudder!' (brother). He chose a role for himself which he felt was acceptable – being the baby was not! He expressed his thoughts. He communicated effectively.

BUILDING SELF-ESTEEM

The first six years of a child's life are highly formative and greatly determine his self-concept (the way he sees himself).

Encouraging independence

The more children are able to do for themselves, the more competent they feel. Their physical skills are limited and this in itself causes frustration. They strive to be independent, but may not be able to cope with tasks like fastening shoes or putting on a jacket. Help children towards independence by making the

environment you are working in as user friendly as possible. Have equipment prepared from the outset, so that they don't always have to ask you for help. Teach them skills like washing hands and unbuttoning cardigans. Let them help *you* with mixing paint or putting out equipment. Encourage parents to dress children so that they can cope with fastenings on their own as far as possible. Imagine your own frustration if you couldn't go to the toilet without having to ask someone to undo your dungarees! Shoes with Velcro straps are easy for young children to manage. The more they can do for themselves, the more they will feel in control of their world.

If children are too young to cope physically with a skill, it will only increase their frustration to be expected to do so. For example, the average six-year-old will enjoy the challenge of learning to tie his own shoe laces, but the three-year-old will become upset because he doesn't yet have the fine-muscle control and co-ordination to cope with this task. Boredom, reluctance to participate or aggressive behaviour are often signs that a child is unable to meet the demands put upon him. Aim to provide activities that children can manage independently. If a task requires an adult's help before a child can complete it, then that task is too difficult for his age group.

Building confidence

Melissa sits struggling to do a jigsaw puzzle. She tries to force a piece into the wrong place. The onlooking adult hisses, 'No, silly!' The child gets the message that she is incompetent.

If a child repeatedly receives this type of negative feedback, she will try to avoid challenges for fear of failure. Every child needs a task that is adequately stimulating but simple enough for her to cope with. If the adult had encouraged Melissa to chat about the jigsaw picture, to look carefully and to try something different, or if he had praised her for completing the task, she would have developed self-confidence and become more willing to accept challenges. In everyday interaction with children we have the opportunity to help them realise their God-given potential.

When children successfully complete a challenge, they experience satisfaction even if no one is around to praise them, and their feeling of competence grows.

Providing opportunities for creativity

Creative materials such as paint, playdough and crayons are all part of the child's world, and it's a world he wants to explore. When we impose our ideas on children, we prevent them from making their own discoveries and realising their own potential. It is far more valuable for them to enjoy the experience of creativity and to learn from it than to have a perfectly crafted product to take home. For example, you have been talking about apples and you want the children to make or draw one, your involvement should only go as far as providing the red paint, crayons or playdough for them to use. If you say 'No, not like that' and try to do it for them, or give them photocopies of an apple to colour in, they will perceive that their creation is not acceptable. Their indecipherable red splashes across the paper are far more valuable than a teacher-drawn apple. They will only realise their ability to express themselves if they are given the opportunity to do so.

Creative activities have great value in building children's self-concept. Ensure that they know you approve of their efforts by offering praise and displaying the results on the walls of your meeting room. This will send a strong message that you value what they have done.

Recognising the child as an individual

It is important to know the names of the children in your group. Our names are a big part of our identity: when we are called by name, we feel we have been noticed.

Learning names is largely a matter of self-discipline. Pin labels on each child and on yourself when your group first meets together, so that everyone's name is visible (don't forget to remove the labels when the children leave at the end of the session). Use mental links to help you remember. Some characteristic may remind you of someone else with the same name.

Read through your list of names at home before the next meeting. Pray over each one and try to envisage that child. At the next meeting, play a simple game that reinforces your memory of names: for example, sitting in a circle and chanting each person's name twice, clapping the syllables at the same time. This helps the children learn each other's names as well.

Anti-bias

Accepting oneself, including one's physical appearance, is important for healthy self-esteem. In South Africa we have moved towards understanding and acceptance of different races and cultures within a few short years, and this has caused many of us to take a long, hard look at ourselves. We have developed some jargon to communicate aspects of this transition. We actively work towards creating an environment which encourages an attitude of 'anti-bias', that is, the acceptance of others regardless of sex, colour, age, disability or background. Young children are naturally 'colour blind'. They don't see any significance in the fact that people are different colours. They learn their prejudices from other people, particularly those they live with.

My most amusing experience of 'colour blindness' was when I was working in a newly established nursery school. I had helped the children to learn about themselves by laying each child on a very large sheet of paper and drawing around them. Sifiso was a creative African child whose closest friend was a European. Sifiso used brown to paint the colour of his hands. He then took a pot of pink paint and began to use this to paint in the face of his 'self-portrait'.

'Sifiso,' I asked, 'what colour is your face?'

'Pink,' he replied. He had not had the opportunity to see himself in the mirror and presumed his face was the same colour as his friend's!

Many of us are unaware of our 'Eurocentric' attitudes. Until very recently, dolls, posters and books generally portrayed 'white' people. By using equipment that represents all race groups, we give children the message that all people are of equal value. So, when you are using paints or crayons, provide a range of colours that allow each child to match his own skin and hair colour.

Look for opportunities to show children that other cultures have value. You might, for example, discuss corn (known as maize in some countries), and you could do this by setting up an interest table showing how it is cooked in different parts of the world. The table could include popcorn, corn on the cob, soft porridge, 'mealie bread' and 'pap'– all made from corn but prepared in various ways by people of different cultures. The children could be encouraged to touch, smell and taste the different forms (cornmeal is available now in many supermarkets). This would give them the opportunity to appreciate the diversity of other cultures, yet also to see that there is something they have in common (the food is all made of corn).

Beware of sexist and ageist typecasting. A mechanic isn't always male and a nurse isn't always female. Grannies don't necessarily have white hair, glasses and false teeth! Ensure that your attitudes and the way you communicate affirm the abilities of girls as well as boys. Even the words of songs we are familiar with in church can put people in 'boxes': for example, we have 'Jesus loves the little girls/With their bows and pretty curls/And he loves the little boys/Even though they make a noise!' I for one was a little girl without 'bows and pretty curls'. I was in my element when dressed in shorts and at the top of a tree. Similarly, not all boys are noisy! So avoid songs, stories and pictures that present stereotyped people. Accept each child for what he or she is, and in every part of your programme encourage this same acceptance in the children.

Encouraging problem-solving skills

Children not only learn their attitudes from their caregivers, they also find out how to converse. A family that tends to communicate in short, stilted sentences will rear children who do likewise, whereas a family that encourages rich, stimulating conversation will rear children who are competent at expressing themselves. Strong verbal skills enable children to make themselves understood and to reason things out. Through interacting with others and playing with toys, they develop the skills necessary for problem-solving. For example, when a 'house' they are building falls down, they will try to find a way to rebuild it so that it can stand. They will attempt different solutions and discuss the problem among themselves. Perhaps they will rebuild it differently. They learn to try different options, to negotiate, to accept alternatives. This is an integral part of the learning process. Your role as caregiver is simply to offer encouragement and support. You are not there to do the task for the children, but to gently guide them to finding their own solutions. As we have seen, when children can solve problems on their own, their self-confidence increases.

AN ATMOSPHERE OF LOVE AND ACCEPTANCE

Children want to know they are loved and special. They are still learning and need some way of measuring how they are doing. Approval is a part of indicating to them that they are 'on the right track'. Look for opportunities to affirm children – a smile may say more than words, and our body language will confirm our affirmation. A gentle hand on a child's shoulder will let him know that I am aware of him. Very often a disruptive child will co-operate in a group if a leader is near enough to hold his hand.

Be sensitive to children's needs. Their body language will indicate when it is time to change an activity. They will become restless if a story is too long, or boisterous if there is nothing challenging to do. Perhaps you have just finished a lively game and you wish to tell the story. Children need time to 'wind down'. A few quiet songs or action rhymes will help slow the pace and tune the children into a calmer activity. Use a soft, soothing tone of voice yourself if you want to create a restful atmosphere. If there are children who won't settle, it is better to go over quietly and fetch them than to sit and bellow at them to join the group. Develop a calm, caring atmosphere.

Dealing with conflict

Sometimes upsets occur and children get angry or cry. Difficult situations need to be handled with care. Once children are old enough to verbalise adequately, they can be encouraged to understand their own feelings. If Jamie and Roald begin fighting over a toy, I intervene immediately to ensure that no one is hurt. I speak quietly with both boys if necessary, perhaps with my arm around a waist or my hand on a shoulder, until they have calmed down. Then I ask them to tell me what happened. I help them to see that they are both feeling unhappy, and encourage them to resolve the conflict through negotiation. They may decide to fetch another car, or to work together to build a garage. Children don't enjoy fighting, and they learn to avoid conflict by developing acceptable social skills.

Dealing with stress

Life can be stressful for young children. There is so much to learn, so many expectations from 'big people' and so many frustrations when they cannot do things themselves. They need gentle reassurance to cope. Laughter is a great stress-reliever, so look for opportunities to have fun together. But always laugh *with* a child and never at him. Seek to create an atmosphere where children feel contented, where they can make friends, in which they are accepted and nurtured towards responsible adulthood.

> Like guides, we walk at times ahead of our students, at times beside them, and at times we follow their lead. In sensing where to walk lies our art. For as we support them toward their best, and cast light on the path ahead, we do so in the name of our respect for their potential and our care for their growth. *(D A Doloz)*

Chapter 5

A place to play

I began in children's ministry as an eager but inexperienced fourteen-year-old, with a love for children but probably little else to my credit! My one clear memory of those early days was the room in which we met. It was small and dark, with a few wooden benches, and dimly lit by a couple of high windows. The outbuilding was tucked away at the back of the church premises. It was certainly not ideal, yet I have fond memories of the times the children and I shared in those imperfect surroundings. They say that ignorance is bliss and perhaps so, because I don't remember feeling at all worried about the inadequacy of our situation at the time!

Perhaps you identify with my description of the far-from-perfect meeting room. Often it seems that those in leadership in the church are out of touch with the needs of young children. I am aware that if I were to find myself in such conditions now, I would certainly make more effort to find suitable accommodation.

A SUITABLE ROOM

If you are clear in your own mind about your requirements, you will probably find it easier to persuade the church leadership to try to meet them. The children's room may not necessarily be a high priority on their agenda (though more and more churches *are* becoming aware of the importance of children's ministry). I learned this the hard way several years ago. Our children's group was crammed into one tiny room, where even action songs had to be limited. If we swung our arms too enthusiastically, we bumped the walls or one another! We kept hoping a new, larger room would be built. To my amazement one day, I walked into the church building to find brand new carpeting had been laid. I was horrified that all this money had been spent when it was obvious that the children's need was so great.

Then I stopped and thought it through. We had presumed that the church leaders realised how desperate we were for more space, but we hadn't made sure that they did. While we had kept hoping for more comfortable accommodation, the decision-makers sitting in the pews had noticed a few threadbare patches of carpet. They had been quite unaware of the cramped conditions a short distance away. I realised then that it's no use bewailing what we don't have: it's much better to excite people about children's ministry and to enthuse them into being concerned about our needs.

Let's envisage a possible scenario so that we can work through some of the practical issues involved in setting up a suitable room. You are about to embark on your ministry for young children. The church elder shows you into a stark, empty room: 'Here it is – it's yours.' Where do you begin?

Preferably one step back! As we have just seen, the choice of the room may have been given little consideration, so right from the start try to involve the leadership in determining the needs of the children. Consider the following factors.

Size

Ideally the room should be large enough for children to move about in freely (about 1.5 m sq for each child).

On the other hand, too large a room can be overwhelming. Sean is a three-year-old who has just started in our younger age group. He has never been away from his parents before. He needs this new, strange environment to give him a feeling of being safe. It must have enough space to move about in, yet be small enough to feel 'like home'.

A room of about 40 m sq is a good size. If a bigger room is the only option, use dividers to section off a suitable portion (large cardboard boxes can be painted and cut so that the sides can be folded out and joined together concertina-style). Preferably this portion will be very near to the entrance so that children don't have to experience walking through a cavernous room before arriving in their 'safe place'.

Proximity

Sean is his young mother's first child and it's a big step for both of them to be apart. She likes to be close by in the church, where we can easily call her, although it hasn't been necessary to do so. Like most children, Sean's 'crocodile tears' dry up as soon as his mother is out of sight. But we are aware that both Sean and his mother feel more comfortable knowing they are not too far apart from each other!

Ideally, the children's room should be close enough for parents to be able to pop out of a church service to check if their children are coping. However, you want to be sufficiently distant from other worshippers to feel relaxed about the noise level. Children need to chatter as they work: talking with each other about what they are doing, what they did at home last night and what they are learning about are all important to their development. The whole experience of being in the group is meaningful for them, and conversation, laughing and singing are a natural part of that experience.

Another important consideration is easy access to the toilets. These should be as close as possible, but if they are some distance away you will need someone to look after the child who 'needs to go' while you continue working with the rest of the group.

Safety

'Prevention is better than cure' is nowhere more important than when working with pre-schoolers. Young children love to explore and to see 'what will happen if…' – like using the scissors on somebody's hair or clothing! Such situations can cause amusement and sometimes embarrassment. We had a short-haired brunette who lopped off her friend's long, blonde locks and tried to stick them onto her own head!

Be continually watchful that children's curiosity doesn't lead them into danger. Make sure they cannot run out onto a road. Remember too that children can be adept climbers! Regularly check your meeting room and play-area for any sign of worn or broken equipment that could cause injury. Check electrical points and fittings, safety bars on high windows, and any other potential dangers such as broken panes of glass or tiles which may cut little fingers. Ensure that there are no poisons (eg paints, household cleaning materials) within reach.

One of the most important rules in child care is *never* leave children unsupervised. If you all leave your meeting room to go somewhere else, like the playground, keep them together in a group and walk in front. Try to anticipate possible accidents and intervene before disaster strikes. A child is quite capable of eating tablets, drinking poison or putting small objects in his nose or ears. Two-year-old Gary ended up with both arms and legs swathed in bandages after he had pulled a chair to the cupboard and reached for a bottle of Benzene which he then threw on the fire. Fortunately, though they were extensive, the burns weren't too severe and he made a good recovery. Ideally, have no dangerous chemicals on the premises, but if you do, make sure they are locked away. Always be on the alert for possible dangers. In the unhappy event of an accident, keep calm, take appropriate action, reassure the child and seek expert advice immediately. It's a good idea to do a basic First Aid course so you are confident you know how to react in an emergency situation.

It may sound as though the potential hazards of working with small children are quite enormous! But in nearly sixteen years of teaching, I can remember only two or three incidents that needed minor medical assistance. If we consciously try to create a safe environment, accidents are less likely to happen.

A pleasant room

Besides looking for a safe environment, try to find a room that won't be too hot in summer or too cold in winter. Easy access to a safe garden area is an advantage, as is running water for use in the preparation of messy activities such as painting, as well as for cleaning up.

You probably won't find the 'perfect room', but many obstacles can be overcome. A bright coat of paint and good lighting will help offset a lack of natural sunshine; heaters or fans will keep the room at a comfortable temperature; and water can always be carried in a bucket (never leave a container of deep water where a child may fall in; rather, put it onto a stable, high surface where it is out of reach). A carpet provides a comfortable surface on which the children can sit for activities such as singing and storytelling.

SETTING UP

The leaders have given you their blessing to use the room. You have ensured that it's safe and have brightened it up. Now what?

Planning the layout

You will help foster feelings of security in the children if, as far as possible, the layout of your room always remains the same. Spend time at the beginning planning this carefully, then try to keep to your original arrangement. All this, of course, depends on your being able to keep your equipment permanently on-site. I'm aware that this isn't always possible, and that the room where the children's ministry takes place is often shared with other church groups or used for other activities. Leaders often have to adapt to suit their circumstances.

Ideally, the room should have separate areas in which the children can play or work at individual activities. The simple outline of these areas given below may help. Try drawing a plan of the room on graph paper, marking fixtures such as doors, windows, basins, and so on. Cover this with a transparent sheet and, with a non-permanent marker, draw in where you plan to put furniture and equipment. This will help you consider your options without having to break your back moving heavy equipment. If you haven't spent any time in a good nursery school, try to arrange to visit one and look out for the aspects outlined here.

Create dividers between the different sections of the play-room. Ideally, these should be above the children's eye-level, so that they can enjoy the experience of being in 'little rooms', but the leader is still able to keep an eye on their activities in all areas. You can create dividers in the following ways:

- Buy or make a specially designed piece of furniture which 'doubles' as something else, for example, a pen-board on one side and shelves on the other for storing art materials or imaginative play-equipment. If the room is used for other purposes during the week, join the two sections with piano hinging and set them on small wheels, so that the two ends can be closed together, securing all your equipment.

- Open up large cardboard boxes, cut, paint and 'sew' them together with strips cut from stockings or tights.

- Use low sections of wooden or plastic fencing secured at the ends by attaching the fencing to large tins filled with sand or cement.

- Erect low curtains, and hold them in place at each end with curtain wire attached to firm wooden poles standing in tins of sand or cement.

Ring area

This is where the children gather to sing, listen to stories and do other things that involve the whole group.

Create a family atmosphere by sitting the children in a semi-circle, all looking towards the leader. If there are too many to sit comfortably in a semi-circle, make a double row with the taller children at the back so that everyone can see clearly. If you sit in a full circle, the children sitting next to the leader won't be able to see his face or any visual aids he is using – particularly important during stories and when learning new songs. It is usually more convenient to have children sitting on the floor on a clean mat or carpet (moving chairs around can be disruptive). The leader should sit on a low chair so that his eye-level is only slightly above that of the children and they can easily see him.

Make sure the children are facing away from any possible distractions. Don't have a window behind the leader, or they will be watching passers-by when you want them to be concentrating on the story! And don't have a wall behind that is so colourful and busy it is a distraction. Go for a calm, uncluttered background. Remember that this is where you will be drawing the children's attention to God. Establish a focus for worship using an attractive plain cloth over a table, with a Bible placed on it (not a pictorial children's Bible, but one that symbolises the authority of God's word). Include other symbols of worship, such as the offering box or perhaps some fresh flowers.

Only the person who is actively leading the group time should be seated at the front. Other leaders and helpers should be sitting among the children, helping them to feel secure and quietly maintaining discipline.

Quiet corner

This is where books may be read and quiet games played. Often the ring area can double as the quiet corner. At the side, provide a bookshelf or a table on which attractive books are laid out, and scatter some cheerful cushions so that children can sit and relax. You may also like to have a display of objects and pictures related to the theme for the day. If possible, have a good magnifying glass on hand so that children can examine interesting objects such as moths, material or skin.

It is important to have a storage cupboard or at least some strong boxes in which you can pack away equipment. Don't put all the quiet area toys out every week. Young children find it easier to pick something when the choice isn't too wide. A small variety of activities, such as jigsaw puzzles and simple games, will be fine. A toy which the children haven't seen for a few weeks will be welcomed as 'new' when it reappears.

Art area

Ideally the flooring in the art area should be washable. If it isn't, lay a large sheet of plastic or sheets of newspaper on the floor when a messy activity is going on.

Children need to be given a choice of creative activities. Like all of us they have different likes and dislikes, and will benefit most from an activity if they have chosen it themselves. Arrange tables so that they can work in groups (a maximum of eight in each group). Remember, tables and chairs should be at a comfortable height for children: don't expect them to work at adult-height tables.

It is good for children to experience working in different body positions. You might have playdough or a cut-and-glue activity on a mat on the floor; a table to stand and paint at; and another table where they can sit and do puzzles or some other activity. (If only a few children are seated at tables at any one time, you will save floor space.)

Try to arrange equipment so that the children are able to do as much as possible for themselves. For instance, the pairs of scissors, crayons, and so on, can all be put ready for them to help themselves to what they need. A simple stand for pairs of scissors may be made by up-turning an egg-box, making a hole through each segment and painting the whole thing with enamel paint – one pair of scissors goes into each hole. Remember to provide only round-ended scissors that cannot cause any injuries.

There should be a place for everything so it is easy to find. When children know where to get what they need, they feel more confident about offering to help prepare and pack away, and they learn to take on responsibility. I have a few children who arrive at school much earlier than the others, and they know they are free to take out and use crayons, scissors, glue, paper, playdough and any of the toys that are in the locker. They

enjoy not having to sit and wait for an adult, but getting on with things for themselves.

Quite often a couple of the 'early birds' choose to help me prepare the equipment. Mixing the paint is always a firm favourite! This is of great help to me, as I can carry on with other duties knowing they are happily busy. By having prepared activities I can spend time with a child or a parent, knowing the rest of the group are occupied. But, more importantly, the children develop self-confidence and a sense of independence as they choose what they wish to do.

Imaginative-play area

This area could be laid out as a 'kitchen' or 'lounge' to make it feel like home, the place children are most familiar with. Children develop language and an understanding of the world through 'acting out' what they know: this gives them an opportunity to come to terms with problems they may be facing. I once observed a little girl pretending to force-feed a doll she had placed in the high chair, eventually screaming at it, 'Eat your food!', and smacking the doll's face! My heart went out to that child as I realised the stressful home situation she was re-enacting (her mother, a single parent, was battling to raise two children, the other mentally disabled). We often have an opportunity to discover something of children's home situations when we watch their imaginative play. This insight will enable us to be more understanding towards children who seem 'difficult'.

Imaginative play also gives children the opportunity to work through feelings in a socially acceptable manner. The little girl could express her anger by smacking the doll, but she knew she wasn't allowed to hit other children. Perhaps boys have an even greater need for this type of play than girls. In our society, where the idea that 'big boys don't cry' may inhibit them from expressing their emotions, imaginative play is a good way of venting pent-up feelings. So it's important that this area is attractive to boys as well as girls. Include small jackets, waistcoats, hats and any other props that will encourage boys to feel welcome.

Give children the opportunity to try out roles they want to explore. Lebo was a stocky little boy in my nursery school class, who delighted in dressing up – in necklaces, dresses, bangles, hats and whatever else caught his imagination. He took the part of a Zulu warrior with great gusto in our annual concert! Children need the freedom to explore different roles, to 'try out being 'Mum' as well as 'Dad'. So if a boy wants to put on a dress, necklace and ladies' shoes, let him. He won't become disoriented about his identity if he does. If a child pretends to be a wolf or a lion in an imaginary game, we don't worry that he will start thinking of himself as a wild animal! Rather, role-play serves to develop self-knowledge and an understanding of who others are in relationship to ourselves. Perhaps if we didn't 'forbid' boys to play with baby dolls, they might find it easier to be nurturing fathers later on!

You may like to make or ask people to donate props for the imaginative-play area. Useful things are dressing-up clothes (including hats, handbags, small briefcases, jewellery and shoes), baby dolls (with suitable accessories such as dolls' clothing, prams, bedding), toy telephones, a small table, a chair, and plastic crockery and cutlery. Make sure jewellery is safe: avoid anything sharp or small enough to be swallowed. Shoes should have low heels that won't be dangerous. Dolls shouldn't be adult dolls but baby ones that encourage a nurturing instinct. Try to have brown dolls as well as white, to develop children's awareness that people of all colours are equally beautiful.

Toy telephones must look like the 'real thing' – old telephones are even better! Telephones help in the formation of communication skills by encouraging children to speak in complete sentences. Gestures and body language cannot be seen over the phone, so they are motivated to use their vocabulary. It always delights me to 'listen in' to children's imaginary telephone conversations and even to be included in the game. Children enjoy it when 'big people' enter into their imaginative play. However, we need to be careful not to intrude when children are busy.

Provide a stand or suitable container in which clothes and other props may be placed when children have finished playing. If the children are not tending to use the imaginative-play area, it probably needs to be changed or livened up, perhaps just by adding some new props. For example, if the 'house' has lost its appeal, try adding simple items such as empty cartons and clean empty tins (but be careful there are no sharp edges) along with some plastic cutlery, crockery, a large cardboard box for a 'stove' and one or two small pans. This will be likely to 'stir up the pot' and have children busy preparing, serving and eating imaginary meals.

Block-play area

This area can be set up close to the imaginative-play area, as very often the activities in these two areas overlap. Children may decide to use the blocks to build a 'stove' or as 'sausages' in the pan. The block-play area should be situated away from the 'traffic' flow in the room, as children will become frustrated if their carefully constructed buildings are sent flying by another child hurrying to the bathroom. An even floor surface is needed, and a firm carpet will absorb sound. Blocks should be regular geometric shapes of all sizes, ideally made from natural, varnished wood. Props like small plastic cars and farm animals can add variety. If wooden blocks aren't available, collect suitable cardboard boxes, fill them with tightly packed newspaper or polystyrene chips, seal the boxes and paint them, or cover them with coloured plastic adhesive paper.

OUTDOOR PLAY

You may have a suitable area to use for outdoor play. First and foremost, ensure that it is safe. I remember a delightful, diminutive two-year-old boy in my group, Luca, who didn't seem able to comprehend that if he walked under the swing or in front of an oncoming tricycle he would be bumped. He also didn't realise the consequences of throwing handfuls of sand into other children's faces. I needed to be continually watching him, ready to intervene to stop him from moving into a 'danger zone' or to enforce basic rules. As he was still too young to understand an explanation of cause and effect, I just told him firmly 'No, Luca!' whenever the handful of sand was about to be tossed. This soon had the desired effect. Establish simple rules to make sure children don't hurt one another. Play-equipment like swings should be made from 'soft' materials (eg car tyres) that won't seriously hurt children if they are bumped.

Always check that the environment is safe *before* the children arrive to play. Earlier this year I found a mole snake in our sand-pit! In rural South Africa, it could just as easily have been a harmful snake. Make sure cats haven't soiled the sand and no broken glass or sharp objects have been introduced. Equipment must be in good repair and user friendly. The 'SAFE' acronym (Secure Alert Free Equipped) may help you to remember the key safety concerns:

Secure

Children should be prevented from going to dangerous areas like roads, high areas (from which they may fall) or near containers of water (a young child can drown in very shallow water).

Alert

The leader must be present at all times, looking out for anything that could threaten the children's safety.

Free

The environment should be free from dangerous objects such as chemicals, poisonous plants, broken glass or sharp objects.

Equipped

Equipment should be in good repair. Check particularly for wear and tear, such as at the joints of swings. Make sure there are no hard or sharp edges.

Outdoor equipment

An outdoor area offers opportunities for children to develop their large-muscle skills. If the area is large, you may want to consider having equipment such as swings and low climbing frames.

A sandpit

This is a must for outdoor play. Even if you don't have a garden, a sand-tray is a valuable resource to have indoors if there is adequate space. Ensure that the sand is clean and fresh. An outdoor sandpit must have a cover over it whenever it is not in use (to prevent soiling from cats). Every few months a generous quantity of coarse salt should be added to combat any germs. Dampen the sand sometimes as this changes its consistency and encourages the children to explore its potential – dry sand is good for pouring, but wet sand is lovely for making moulds. It is worth buying a few strong plastic spades, rakes and buckets for sand-play, but if you are on a tight budget basic shapes can be cut from old plastic containers that have been thoroughly cleaned. If edges are rough and sharp, use the heat from a candle to melt these away (do this at home, and not with children around).

Water-play

Children love playing with water. They must always be closely supervised, and water should be in a shallow container raised to their waist height. As some spilling is inevitable, only have water-play when weather conditions are favourable.

Ensure that any long sleeves are rolled up, and remove excess layers of clothing such as cardigans or jumpers. Ideally, use small plastic aprons to keep clothes dry. Collect suitable bottles for pouring, squirting and measuring. Children love to see water squirting out from multiple holes in the base of a plastic container (make these by piercing holes with a heated skewer or large nail).

Vary water-play on different days by using any of the following ideas:

- Add food colouring to the water.
- Add large blocks of ice, but don't let children put these in their mouths – there is a risk of choking.
- Add dish-washing liquid and sponges.
- Add dish-washing liquid, egg-beaters and whisks.
- Provide measuring cups and funnels (funnels can be made from the top half of a plastic bottle).

Small apparatus

To develop children's skills and to provide amusement, a variety of small apparatus can be bought or made:

- Large, soft balls are most suitable for small hands, and these can be made out of old tights or stockings stuffed with scraps of material.

- Beanbags made to a size that fits comfortably in a child's hand. Use a variety of colours of material and fill the bags with cat litter (the traditional beans have a bad habit of growing if they become moist!). Don't overfill a beanbag – it needs to be flexible so that it can be held properly.

- A variety of coloured hoops are good for all sorts of games.

- Plastic bottles make good skittles when they are weighted with a small quantity of sand or plaster of Paris poured into the base (they must still be easy to bowl over). Use your imagination when you decorate them with paint!

- Pom-pom catchers are easily made by cutting the base off plastic containers with handles. A large pom-pom is attached to each container, opposite the handle, by a short length of elastic (about 30 cm). Each child can then hold a container by the handle and try to flick the pom-pom into it.

- A pair of sturdy tins, about 10–20 cm high, make fun 'walking tins' – children stand on these and use them like low stilts. Pierce a hole on either side of each tin, and thread through a length of thin rope. Knot this at the ends inside the tin, so that the child can stand on the tins and hold the rope at waist height. He then uses the rope to lift the tins as he 'walks'.

- Simple racquets can be made by reshaping a wire coathanger and covering it with a stocking. Use insulation tape to cover the wire handle securely. Use the racquets to knock about sponge balls, pom-poms or soft balls made out of stockings or tights.

SOME REMINDERS

The room in which I first started in children's ministry nearly thirty years ago was certainly not the perfect environment for young children. But I like to think that the memories those children have are as warm as my own. The environment we work in may not be the best, but we can still make it a special place where Jesus' love is always present.

Consider all the possibilities, and seek to create an environment that encourages children to feel that this is a fun place to be. Consider their safety. Always have some familiar activities like playdough or block-play. Children enjoy the stimulation of new equipment, but like the safety of the familiar. Don't flood them with new activities every week: instead, introduce one new activity at a time alongside two or three familiar ones.

Allow children at an activity according to the quantity of equipment available: for example, if there are only eight pairs of scissors, have only eight children doing a cutting-activity. Encourage others to do something else until there is a space at the cutting table.

You may not have all the equipment you want when you start, but over a period of time you will be able to build up your stock. Make a list and start collecting what you need. At present the nursery school I work in is planning to set aside a morning to make small apparatus for outdoor play. We will start with a bring-and-share cooked breakfast (to attract parents to join). Several planning meetings with a subcommittee are in progress to ensure that we have all the tools and materials ready. An example or clear diagrams of each type of small apparatus is to be provided. By the time we reach 'D-Day' we will have all the necessary equipment and resource materials laid out, with a facilitator at each workstation so that everyone concerned will immediately be able to use their time constructively.

An idea well worth considering is to make contact with a

retirement home or senior citizens' club, and to ask if they would be willing to help make equipment. Very often there are older people with many skills who would love the opportunity to contribute to a worthy cause. But do give clear directions on what you require, taking into account the abilities and resources of the people concerned.

Not every room will provide ideal storage, but at least try to have a cupboard in which your equipment can be safely stored. Collect regular-sized boxes, such as apple or photocopier paper boxes, and coat them with enamel paint. Have a suitable box prepared and labelled for each type of equipment, so that you can quickly unpack whatever you need. It's important to look after equipment and to store it carefully. Have containers with picture labels stuck on them that children can easily identify, such as a picture of a beanbag on the beanbag container, a picture of a skittle on the skittle container, and so on. Encourage children to help with setting up and packing away: this engenders responsibility and caring for their environment.

Remember that a pre-school environment should be a prepared environment. Every day I plan my programme so that everything is ready and the children can get involved without having to wait for the leader's help.

Try to be present at least half an hour before the children arrive, to prepare the room and to pray together as a team. Our ministry is just as important as that of the minister or any other leader in the church – the Christian witness to those little ones is our responsibility. By the time the children arrive, the leaders should be ready to give their attention wholly to the children, and not be dashing around trying to locate glue or chatting to friends!

You never get a second chance at a first impression. As the young child comes into the environment we have prepared, what will his first impression of Christianity be? I pray that he will think:

'This is a safe place.'

'I feel loved and cared for.'

'This is a fun place to be!'

Chapter 6

The Bible and the young child

Johnny came home from Sunday group very excited. His mother asked him what he had learned that day, and he enthusiastically told her about Moses crossing the Red Sea. He started detailing the events: 'They used helicopters to airlift the people to the other side, and then they used jet fighters to chase after the king...'

'That's not really what your leader told you, is it?' asked his mother, concerned.

'Mom,' he exclaimed, 'if you heard what she told us, you wouldn't believe it either!'

The Bible is an incredible book with wonderful stories – it's easy to appreciate children's difficulty in grappling with it. We need to consider how we can present it in a form they can grasp.

Our children are growing up in a world that is often sceptical about the Christian faith. Our goal is to nurture within them a love for God's word and a capacity to trust it. A report by Terry Clutterham captures the essence of this involvement:[1]

> Bible stories answer the basic question of Christian belief: what is it like to be a believer in a world that is hostile to the way God exercises his Lordship on earth? So an exposure to them (and to the shape of the whole story of the Bible) is very important, to enable children to identify with the people of the story and to make it their story both at community and individual level.

Story tells us who we are, and can help us to (re)capture the mystery and excitement of a relationship with God.

DIFFICULTIES WITH THE BIBLE

Young children aren't fluent readers and have to rely on adults to share the Bible with them. The Bible wasn't written for children, so neither its vocabulary, nor its sentence structure, nor its literary phrases are easily followed by the pre-schooler or early reader. Very often he will try to put his own interpretation on words he doesn't understand. A friend's child came home to tell his mother that his headmaster's name was Harold. The mother enquired how he knew this. He replied, 'Every morning he stands up and says, "Our Father who is in heaven, Harold is my name..."'

The Bible was written in another time about another culture. The lifestyle and geographical conditions portrayed are far removed from the experience of children today, particularly children in the West. They cannot envisage a world without information technology, in which the way of life, the landscape, even the animals, are unfamiliar. Another difficulty is that many of the stories in the Bible are violent, and record events and details unsuitable for the ears of young children. My brother, at about the age of ten, became an avid reader of the Bible. My mother asked him if he was enjoying it. 'Oh yes,' he enthused. 'It's full of stories about battles and killing!'

THE CHILD'S NATURE

However, some aspects of the young child's nature make him receptive God's word: Jesus himself acknowledged this (Matt 18:3). Children are naturally trusting and open. They don't have the veneer that adults develop to camouflage their true selves. They believe what they are told. They love to make discoveries, and their natural curiosity is insatiable. They have vivid imaginations that will allow them to enter a world they have never

experienced. The challenge of presenting the Bible to young children lies in creating ways of helping them understand it.

A colleague shared her interpretation of the story of Jesus and Peter meeting on the beach after the resurrection. Jesus tells Peter first to 'Feed my lambs', then to 'Feed my sheep' (John 21:15-17). My friend pointed out that although lambs actually receive the same type of nourishment as sheep (it comes from the same nutrient), it is 'served' in a predigested form that is more assimilable for baby animals. Our 'lambs' should receive the same form of spiritual nourishment as adults do, but it needs to be prepared and presented in a more digestible form.

Although the Bible wasn't written for children, there are many suitable stories or verses we can introduce to them. Using language they understand, we can present scripture in a way that allows children to interact with the text and to relate it to their own life-world experience.

REACHING THE CHILD THROUGH THE SENSES

God created our senses, and he intended that we should grow in our understanding of him through them. From the earliest times God used natural 'story aids' to focus our attention on him. Think of some of the visual images presented in the Bible – the rainbow, the pillars of cloud and fire, even the cross itself. The people who witnessed Elijah's challenge to the prophets of Baal not only saw the fire burning the sacrifice, they no doubt smelled and heard it too (1 Kings 18:16-46). They felt the long-awaited rain lashing their bodies.

Through creation God uses our senses to heighten our awareness of him and to assure us of his concern for us. This weekend my husband preached at the worship service celebrating the annual Cherry Blossom Festival, when the Haenertsberg region in South Africa is flooded with sensuous pinks, reds and mauves of blossom cascading from the cherry trees and azalea bushes. I am always overwhelmed by its beauty. You may experience something similar at the sight of a meadow of flowers, a wood in autumn or the evening sky. It is impossible to see such magnificence without being overawed by the thought of God's love for *me*. Look for opportunities to increase children's learning experience by appealing to their senses.

Children need to look, touch and explore in order to make every experience meaningful. Imagine a child who has never had a go on a playground slide being shown a picture and told 'This is a slide'. Just because he has seen a picture of it won't mean that he *knows* a slide. But when he has climbed the metal rungs, felt the twinge of fear of standing up so high at the top, experienced the exhilaration of whizzing down the smooth metal surface and repeated the whole thrilling process over and over again — then the child *knows* a slide. His 'hands-on' experience has given him a concept of it. Then, when he sees a picture of a slide, it will be meaningful to him. He needs to be able to relate new things to the knowledge and practical experience he already has.

When presenting unfamiliar Bible material, find ways of linking it with things the children know, so that it will have meaning. If I tell the story of the manna in the desert, I use food similar to unleavened bread such as pitta bread spread with honey, to give them an idea of the food God provided. I encourage them to feel it, to look at it, to smell and taste it.

Festival occasions

Another way of bringing the Old Testament to life for children is to focus on the festivals it describes. Some years ago I served as principal of a Jewish nursery school. While I was there I came to appreciate the richness of the Hebrew tradition of celebrating the great biblical events. These occasions give families the opportunity of remembering the wonderful things God has done for his people. They are marked with special foods and festivities similar to those we have at Christmas and Easter. Purim is based on the book of Esther, and celebrates how Queen Esther and her uncle, Mordecai, persuaded King Ahasuerus to save the Hebrew people from Haman's wicked plot. Sweetmeats are eaten (sometimes nicknamed 'Haman's ears') and fancy-dress and hats are worn. We used to have a hat-making competition, providing all sorts of scrap materials and encouraging the children to devise their own creations. Succoth (the Feast of Booths) is a form of harvest festival, celebrating God's provision. Hanukkah (the Feast of Lights) celebrates the re-lighting of the lamp in the temple by Judas Maccabaeus in 165BC.

Perhaps you know someone Jewish who would be happy to share recipes and other ideas to help you mark these occasions from the Old Testament. Festivals give us the opportunity to celebrate God's goodness to us. God is saying to us, 'Let's have a party!'

Learning through activity

Children's naturally high energy level means they will benefit from a programme which gives them plenty of opportunity for active involvement. Art, mime, dance and song can all be used to draw children to an experience of the biblical text. Scripture Union's SALT resources are excellent for helping to present God's word to children, not only through Bible stories but also through songs, memory verses, ideas for prayer, praise activities, and so on. The Bible has many different types of literature besides the narrative and the historical. When we make the most of these different styles in our programmes, we introduce children to the rich variety the Bible has to offer: for example, in *Let's Praise and Pray* (Scripture Union, 1994, p 105) Psalm 104 has been used as the basis for a lively action rhyme:

My God is very great

My *(thumbs up, pointing to self)* God *(thumbs pointing upwards)* is very great!
He gives fire to keep me warm.
(Rub hands together.)

My God is very great!
(Repeat actions.)
He gives water for the donkeys to drink.
(Hands to side of head to make ears.)

My God is very great!
(Repeat actions.)
He gives bread to make me strong.
(Flex muscles in arms.)

My God is very great!
(Repeat actions.)
He plants trees for birds to nest in.
(Stretch arms wide.)

All these things my God has done.
(Move arms in circle.)
Thank you, God, you are very great!
(Clap in rhythm.)

BASED ON PSALM 104
© Elizabeth Alty

The language and subject matter of this poem are easily understandable. The simple actions naturally involve the children, and they will relate happily to the Bible when it's presented in this way.

At times, an appropriate short piece of scripture can be repeated during the programme. For children who cannot read, this could be in the form of a simple chant or an activity involving movement or song. Children who can read will also enjoy this more varied approach. Much fun can be had, for example, popping balloons that have a word from a verse on (or inside) them, having team races or using puppets, to name just a few ideas – there are all sorts of ways to learn a memory verse with children. Avoid singling any one child out to repeat a verse in front of the group. Nervousness may cause her to forget it, and will negate the learning experience for everyone. The key principle is to recite the verse in unison. If you want to see whether individual children have learnt the text, do this individually while the others are involved in something else. It is preferable that children benefit from the total experience and avoid school-like 'testing'.

Dance

Children love to move their bodies expressively. Use your imagination to find creative ways to incorporate dance into the programme. Put on some taped 'praise' music and invite the children to dance to express their love for God. Thin scarves, short streamers or bells attached to ankles or wrists can be used occasionally. For example, if I am working on a water theme, I may use streamers in blues and purple to add to the effect. If celebrating spring, I may use strips of bright floral materials. Children can be exposed to different styles of praise and worship music, to suit the mood of the occasion. When celebrating the triumphal entry into Jerusalem, I use taped 'hosanna' music with the children joining in the refrain and pretending to lay palm branches along the road before Jesus.

Music

Children love to make music. It is worth buying a few well-made percussion instruments with a clear sound. Quality products will last indefinitely if they are carefully looked after. Teach children how to handle them properly, particularly how to pack them away (always supervise this). Have similar instruments stored together in a container or cupboard with a picture of that particular instrument stuck on the outside.

You might like to create a music corner, where children can experiment with the sounds of different instruments. Have enough for at least one-third of the group to play at a time. Every child will want to have an opportunity, so encourage them to take turns.

Young children find it difficult to sing *and* play an instrument simultaneously, so teach them to keep their instruments quiet during some parts of the song and to play only when you give the signal. If the children have had no previous experience with percussion instruments, start simply. In your first session, introduce the instrument, telling the children what it is called, discussing its shape and what it is made of. Demonstrate how to use it and explain how to look after it. Then pass the instrument around, letting each child hold it and try to make a sound with it. Finally, play the instrument yourself, accompanying the children as they sing something they know well. They will see how to handle the instrument correctly. In your next session, remind the children of what you did before, allowing them to take turns at accompanying a song using only that particular type of instrument. Introduce other instruments in similar fashion, one at a time.

If you are not able to purchase instruments, home-made ones can give as much fun, though their life span may be limited. Some ideas include:

- Several bells or metal bottle-tops strung onto elastic or slipped onto a large key ring.

- Plastic bottles, decorated and filled with dry beans in them, to make shakers. Use acrylic glue to seal the lids.

- Short lengths of thick dowel rods for children to clap together. Cut grooves along the sides to give a different sound.

- Wooden blocks with sandpaper glued to the inner surfaces to make a rasping sound.

- Saucepan lids or tin lids to use as cymbals.

- Large tins to use as drums.

You don't have to be a skilled musician to lead music effectively. In fact, a piano is *not* an ideal instrument – it forces the leader to face away from the children. A keyboard is more versatile. Guitars are also good for accompaniment. If you don't play any instrument, you may wish to introduce new tunes by using recorded music. However, children are quite happy to sing along unaccompanied with their leader: if you sing enthusiastically, they will too.

If the children or their families have musical instruments at home, arrange for whoever plays to give a demonstration.

Musical instruments from different cultures can be particularly interesting.

Songs

Besides considering whether or not a song will be meaningful to the children, you need to take account of a number of factors. Children enjoy bright, happy tunes with a regular beat, so avoid those with irregular timing or long notes that are difficult for them to hold (ideally, one beat for each syllable of a word). Songs that start not lower than middle C and which go no more than an octave higher, with only a small range between two succeeding notes, work best.

Always start with at least one or two familiar songs before you teach a new one. Introduce the new song by singing it once or twice to the children. In your next session, sing it again and encourage them to join in. It is better that children learn songs as a whole, rather than broken up line by line. Pre-schoolers find it easier to learn songs with simple, repetitive wording. With older children, a combination of simple words and symbols on OHP transparencies or flip charts will help them learn. You could draw a series of pictures to represent the characters in a song like 'If I were a butterfly'. As you all sing the song, show the picture of the appropriate animal to remind the children of the words.

Children enjoy familiarity, so build up a repertoire of the songs they like. I have a large, re-usable poster in my classroom which has the heading 'Songs and Rhymes', a small picture to brighten it up and regular horizontal lines drawn across it (like a page from an exercise book). I have covered it with transparent adhesive plastic and keep it prominently displayed with a penboard marker next to it. Whenever I teach my group a new song or rhyme that they enjoy, I add the title to the list. If we have a few spare minutes during a session, I can then choose a song or rhyme by simply glancing at the chart.

Many of the songs we sing remind us of God's love and care. Some are based on Bible stories or use words taken directly from the Bible. From time to time, draw children's attention to these words and show them the relevant passage of scripture. Children remember melodies, and music is a wonderful way of teaching them God's word.

Children also enjoy creating their own songs, so try taking a simple, repetitive song like 'Thank you, Lord, for this fine day'; ask them to suggest other things to thank God for, and include these in the song. Older children can be given a theme and left to set their own words to a simple tune such as a nursery rhyme. When my husband was a director of Scripture Union South Africa, we had an inter-primary annual music festival where the Scripture Union group in each school was asked to prepare an item based on a given reading, such as a psalm. Every year we were amazed at the wonderful creativity of song, dance and even rap which the children presented.

Mime and drama

Group mime is an effective way to enact a Bible passage, though young children may need someone to take the lead, at least to start with. Plan mime activities that involve all the children, and use a verse or story script where the children are encouraged to mime spontaneously (ie don't teach them to do specific actions). Older children can handle being given a certain role, but, where possible, involve all members of the group. Avoid singling out the 'best' actors; instead, use the opportunity to encourage everyone to participate.

If you wish to present a special item for an audience, keep it simple – children lose concentration quickly and don't enjoy lengthy practices. Some of the sketches in books by Burbridge and Watts are easy to produce in a comparatively short time, since they rely on a narrator who gives the lead for appropriate mimed responses and sound effects.[2]

Stories

> You and I are not to use the Bible to club a child, or to
> impose demands that he or she conform. We are to use

> Bible stories as gentle words from God: loving words
> spoken by the Holy Spirit, lovingly providing insight and
> hope. We too must be patient and loving and gentle, and
> share helpful Bible stories as a doorway to hope rather
> than a nagging demand for change. *(Larry Richards)*[3]

Simplifying the language of the text makes it possible to introduce many biblical stories to young children. Some can be adapted, leaving the essence of the story intact: for example, children enjoy hearing about Joseph and his 'rags to riches' rise to success: but details of how he was falsely accused by Potiphar's wife can easily be left out. Ensure that stories are simple and straightforward. If there are aspects of a story that are unsuitable but important to the plot, don't use the story.

Besides ensuring that children understand the content of the story, their emotional need for security must be taken into account. In Judges 11:30–40, Jephthah promises God that he will sacrifice to him the first living thing which greets him when he comes home victorious from battle. Imagine a young child's shock at learning that Jephthah sacrificed his daughter. Stories that could make a child feel frightened should be avoided: for example, Abraham's attempt to sacrifice his son; Solomon and the two mothers arguing over a baby,;or the plagues of Egypt. Feelings of anxiety may negate any other value the story may have. Slightly older children may be able to handle such stories if we emphasise the positive rather than dwell on their frightening side. For example, I may tell six-year-olds the story of Daniel in the lion's den or Noah and the ark, but my emphasis will be on the wonderful way in which God saved his people, while I minimise the fearful and gruesome aspects.

One of the biggest challenges is how to deal with the story of Christ's crucifixion, which can so easily be disturbing. If possible, avoid the topic with under fours, who won't have any comprehension of death. However, as Christ's death is central to our faith, we cannot ignore this event. With slightly older children, I mention the crucifixion with little detail. As children have a strong sense of justice, I explain that Jesus was a very good man who loved everybody, and it wasn't fair that some bad men killed him. I immediately move on to the good news that he came back to life. Then the stress of thinking of Jesus suffering is quickly over – children of this age don't yet have the emotional maturity to deal with it.

Some educationalists advocate that Bible stories must remain true to the text. However, I believe that we can use our imaginations to create stories based on the Bible, provided they remain true to the *spirit* of the text. There is a current video in which modern-day children are transported back to Bible times in their time-machine; the children then interact with biblical characters. This way of handling the text may cast doubt on its integrity. There is a danger that the Bible becomes fantasy, on a level with Power Rangers or Superman. Be careful not to misrepresent biblical fact. A pastor told a wildly exciting version of David, desperately grabbing stone after stone from his pouch before eventually killing Goliath. However, this is not in accordance with the account in 1 Samuel 17:49!

However, poetic licence can be used provided the historical and geographical detail of the story remains intact. For instance, I may tell the Christmas story from the viewpoint of the donkey because, as Luke 2:7 records, 'She [Mary] gave birth to her first son, wrapped him in strips of cloth and laid him in a manger – there was no room for them to stay in the inn'. The record in the scriptures and the background situation make it strongly probable that a donkey would have been near to the scene of the birth, so I believe such poetic licence to be acceptable.

When preparing a story, read the Bible text from several different translations, and refer to concordances and other reference books to get a grasp of the historical setting. You want to present as accurate a story as possible, so as not to cause the child to question the validity of the scriptures at a later stage. I personally have grave reservations about introducing young children to the Easter Bunny and Father Christmas or Santa. When children realise that these are fantasy figures and reject them, they may also doubt Bible stories with which they have been associated. I prefer to explain that Santa Claus is derived from St Nicholas, a kind man who gave presents to everyone because he wanted to show them how much God loves them. I make no mention at all of the fictitious Easter Bunny, who has no scriptural basis. But I do use the egg as a reminder that Easter is a special time when we remember that Jesus died on the cross: I break open a hollow Easter egg and explain that it is like the cave where they put Jesus' body when he was dead. It is empty because Jesus came to life again!

In *Children and the Bible*, Rob Cornish states, 'Stories are the soil in which the Gospel takes root.' The farmer knows that a crop isn't harvested in one day. Our role is to prepare the soil by presenting Bible stories in a way that young children can understand. Deeper interpretations will develop as they mature. Recently, I watched a youth pastor give a lovely message to pre-schoolers based on the story of Jesus washing the disciples' feet. He used an effective introduction, having one of the leaders come in with muddy feet. He offered to help and washed the leader's feet clean. The children were easily able to relate to the story of Jesus washing his disciples' feet. Sadly, the pastor tried to take the message further than these young minds could understand by using the story to explain how Jesus washed our sins away. The pre-schooler cannot comprehend such symbolism. Be satisfied with preparing the soil now and trust the Holy Spirit to sow the seed and bring it to fruition in his own good time.

Children like heroes – you only have to think of famous tales such as Robin Hood or Superman to recognise this. They need positive role models, and they will enjoy listening to Bible stories with heroes like Samson or David in them. However, the emphasis of any Bible story should be on God himself. Gideon was a hero, but God gave him the courage to fulfil his mission. Peter and Paul healed the blind man, but only through God's power. Always affirm that *God* is the provider, the carer and the source of the hero's strength.

The Bible is the foundation of our faith, and our teaching

must at all times be based on God's word. However, there is a place for contemporary stories. Jesus himself told these when he used parables. He referred to things and events in people's everyday lives to which they could naturally relate, to help them gain a clearer understanding of what God was like. Children don't have any experience of the world of the Bible: they know only their own immediate environment. By using stories that refer to their world, we give them a 'handle' to hold onto. For example, if the theme is 'God gives water', a story that helps a child realise how she uses water in her everyday life will be significant. We may use both a contemporary story and a Bible story within the same programme. There may be times when we use only the contemporary story, but stress the word of God by using an appropriate passage, such as Psalm 65:9–10.[4] The contemporary story is a valid means to bridge the gap between the child's world and the world of the Bible.

'Thy Word is a lamp unto my path and a light unto my feet' (Psalm 119:105) is Scripture Union's key verse. As guides, we carry the lamp of scripture on behalf of the children in our care until they are old enough to take on that responsibility themselves. A lamp to light the way in the dark saves the traveller from peril and gives him security, hope and comfort along the way.

Notes

1 Terry Clutterham, *Children and the Bible*, Scripture Union, 1992, p 146.

2 P Burbridge and M Watts, *Lightning Sketches* and *Time to Act*, Hodder and Stoughton, 1981.

3 Larry Richards, *Talkable Bible Stories*, Zondervan.

4 Christine Wright, *Jigsaw* Book 1, Scripture Union, 1996, p 31; the theme of 'Water' is a good example of this.

Chapter 7

'Tell us a story'

I love storytelling. It is a great privilege to enthral children with the excitement, colour and action of stories, particularly when these stories are the means of conveying to them the beauty of God's word and the character of their creator. Storytelling is a craft, and like all crafts it improves with training and practice. This chapter outlines some of the practical steps to successful storytelling.

PRINCIPLES OF EFFECTIVE STORYTELLING

Plan the story
A good story has an attention-grabbing introduction, a middle that is packed with incident, and a satisfying ending. Good stories don't just 'happen': they are planned and rehearsed well in advance. After you have decided on a story, practice telling it to the mirror, your pet or a volunteer audience. Use any feedback to improve your technique. Taping yourself can also prove useful.

Settle the children
Seat the children comfortably in a semi-circle, facing you. Position taller children behind the smaller ones. If there is a visually impaired child in the group, make sure that he sits close enough to be able to see the visual aids.

Before you begin, settle the group by using a soothing song or finger rhyme. If there is still some chatter, try saying something like 'Listen quietly now' and wait, keeping still yourself and looking at those causing the disturbance, until all eyes are fixed on you. If you do this regularly, it will become a cue to which the children quickly respond. Any other leaders in the group can help settle a talkative or restless child by placing a calming hand upon him and signalling that this is a time for quiet. If you are aware that particular children tend to 'play up' when they sit together, diplomatically separate them from one another before you begin. As far as possible, prepare the physical environment so as to ensure the children's full concentration on the story.

The introduction

One of the key features of successful storytelling is an effective introduction that captures the children's attention. Once your group is ready, don't waste time with statements like 'Now, children, I have a story to tell you…' – launch in immediately.

Plan the first sentence as an immediate attention grabber. It should introduce the children to the characters and setting of the story. Ideally, it should serve as a bridge from the child's immediate world into the world of the Bible. For example, I might tell the story of Samuel and Eli from the viewpoint of a mouse in the Temple. I start something like this: 'I'm thinking of a teeny weeny animal. It has a soft coat, small round ears, and it makes little squeaky noises. Can you guess what it is?' I then proceed to tell the story, using a mouse puppet or an appropriate set of visual aids. This captures the children's attention because it helps them relate what follows to their life-world. Children are naturally attracted to small creatures. As they identify with the mouse, they are drawn into the story. It provides the necessary springboard to carry them from the world they know to a foreign one.

The middle

Unless they are actively involved, children are likely to concentrate for little more than five to ten minutes – not much time! Make your story-line a simple one, with no deviations or sub-plots that will confuse them. Make the most of your voice and visual aids as you unfold the plot, move smoothly from one key point to the next, and build up to the climax. Eliminate any unnecessary details. The KIS principle always applies – Keep It Simple! Scripture Union's *Jigsaw* material has excellent examples of using uncomplicated stories effectively.

The end

We have all seen films with unsatisfactory endings where the plot seems to have been left 'hanging in the air'. When we tell a story to children, everything should be 'nicely wrapped up' before we finish. Any 'baddies' must have been dealt with and the hero have achieved God's purpose before we can all sit back and relax! Serial stories are not suitable, because young children live in the present – for them, waiting a week or even a day for the story to continue is too long. They are so involved in the immediate, they will probably have forgotten where you are in a story by the time you get round to finishing it.

Suitable language

Always communicate in words that young children comprehend. If they don't understand the vocabulary, they won't understand the story! If there is a word you want to use in the story that the children are unfamiliar with, be sure to explain it simply: for example, if you refer to the Temple in Jerusalem, you could tell them that the people built a special church called 'the Temple'. If you are telling them about Pharaoh, say that he was the king of a very hot, far-away country called Egypt. Only ever use a few unfamiliar words – keep the focus on the story.

Avoid using a word that has two different meanings in the same story. I once heard a story in which 'a well' (of water) and 'getting well' were both mentioned: this may be confusing to children who are still learning language. They enjoy onomatopoeic words, which capture sounds: 'The water whooshed', 'The donkey went trit-trot, trit-trot down the street'. Look for opportunities to use these. Alliteration, where the same sound is repeated, can also be used to good effect: 'The wild waves swirled and swished'. Careful planning of the choice of words greatly enhances a story, particularly when you are describing a dramatic event. Repetition also works well. We only need to think of traditional fairy tales such as the wolf who 'huffed and puffed and blew the house down'. Some stories lend themselves well to this approach, and children enjoy the familiarity of the repeated words or sentences. A story in which a situation occurs a number of times lends itself to devising a catchy line. A good example is the parable of the sower: 'The rain fell, the sun shone and the seeds began to grow and grow'.

Make stories come alive by using direct speech. Rather than 'Jesus told the man to come to him', say 'Jesus said to the man, "Come here." ' Change your voice to take on the speech of each character. Listen to yourself to catch any hesitations or speech 'tics' such as 'um', 'er', 'and' or 'and then'. Work on eliminating any habit that will detract from the atmosphere of the story. If you find yourself frequently saying 'And then...', break this habit by using shorter sentences – this will add vitality to the story.

The most important point to emphasise with storytelling is *tell it*. Don't read it. Talk to the children directly, keeping eye contact with them, using facial and vocal expressions, communicating in a way they understand.

An unusual angle

Children have vivid imaginations. Try to find an unusual perspective, such as telling the story as an animal, one of the onlookers, or the person it is all happening to. Choosing an unusual angle often heightens the intensity of the drama.

Overdramatisation

Be careful not to overdo it. Young children have difficulty distinguishing between reality and fantasy. Dwell on the positive aspects of the story, and minimise or avoid any parts that may be frightening. For example, I may tell the story of Jesus and the storm to children aged six and over, but I avoid making the storm so dramatic that the children become scared. If the story won't make sense after eliminating a fearful part, don't use it.

Avoid interruptions

Ensure that physical needs, like trips to the bathroom, have been dealt with before story-time. If the children were involved in a quiet activity, sing a few action songs before settling them down again.

At times the story will remind a child of something he wants to tell you or ask you. A story loses its vitality when it is stopped in mid-sentence. If some children in your group are inclined to interrupt, tell them before you begin that you want them to listen quietly and you will give them a chance to chat afterwards. Make sure you keep your word, otherwise they will be more hasty to interrupt in future! If a child tries to barge in to the story, hold out your hand in a 'Stop' sign and make eye contact to indicate to him that he mustn't interrupt. It may be necessary to tell an insistent child to wait. Try to keep the story flowing.

Body language

Children will politely tell you when a story isn't capturing their attention. If it's too long, unexciting or above their level of comprehension, they soon begin to fidget. If they are enjoying the story, their attention will be firmly fixed on the storyteller.

Evaluating your storytelling skills will help you identify where you may need to improve. Even though I am an experienced storyteller, there are times when I realise that I am losing the children's attention, perhaps because they are overexcited or overtired. I aim to recapture their interest by changing my tone, pitch or volume, or I bring the story to a quick end. It is probably better to cut a story to the bare minimum than to struggle on regardless of whether the children are taking it in.

EVALUATION

As with all aspects of ministry we need to evaluate ourselves constantly. Ask others for feedback, to help you improve your skills. You may find questions like these useful:

Was the story suitable for the age group?
Did the children understand it?
Was the story a good length?
Was it well prepared?
Was the plot easy to follow?
Did the story hold the children's attention?
Did the storyteller use his/her voice and body language effectively?
Did the storyteller use direct speech?
Did the story satisfy the child's emotional needs (ie was it too frightening, did it have a satisfying conclusion)?
Was the vocabulary suitable for young children?
Did the choice of words enhance the story?
Were any unnecessary words or phrases frequently used?
Did the story flow?
Were suitable story aids used effectively?
Did the children enjoy the story?

Don't just evaluate on the days when things go wrong; evaluate your good stories too. Improve your skills by recognising what works.

THE IMPORTANCE OF PRACTICE

The art of storytelling requires regular, disciplined practice. A few months ago my husband asked me to tell a story in church. I knew I was inadequately prepared, though in the ends things didn't go too badly. My husband commented afterwards, 'You weren't yourself today. I've never seen you glance at your notes before.'

When preparing, I always write down key words to help me remember the story-line. Although I keep these on hand, I have usually practised the story so thoroughly that I don't need to refer to them. My family are quite accustomed to a variety of strange voices coming from the bathtub! Practice is essential. Saturate yourself in a story. Go over it again and again. Remember – you are bringing God's message.

A MULTI-SENSORY APPROACH

As we have seen, young children learn through a multi-sensory approach. Stories may involve not only auditory but also visual and tactile responses – even taste and smell at times!

Body movement

As children are naturally active, the learning experience can be heightened through physical involvement. For example, when I tell the story of Abraham's travels (Gen 12:1-10; 13:12-18), I begin the story with the children sitting in the usual semi-circle. When we come to the part where God tells Abraham to move, we pretend to pack up and trek through the garden to a tree to sit in the shade. There I continue the story until we come to the part where God tells Abraham to move again. We repeat the activity, pretending to pack up, moving through the garden until we reach another suitable place to stop. The story captures the children's imaginations as they become involved in the action. (If your outside space or the weather don't permit, try to use the same approach inside.)

Physical involvement of the children can be used to great effect in a wide range of stories. Another example would be that of Jesus calming the storm. I encourage the children to make appropriate noises for the wind, and to use their arms and rock their bodies to enact the waves (Matt 8:23-27). If we are having a story with soldiers marching or a donkey trotting, we clap our hands on our thighs to create suitable sound effects.

Young children respond well to group mime. I find it best to tell the story first and then use mime as a follow-up activity. (It is important to have enough space for the children to move freely, and to teach them to respond immediately to your 'Stop' signal.) Stories such as the parable of the sower lend themselves well to this (Matt 13:3-8). The children can pretend to be the sower throwing the seed from the bag, then the birds coming down to eat it. They can mime the little seeds that begin to grow, but then wilt and die in the hot sun. They can mime the seeds that grow bigger, but which are then choked by the weeds.

(I don't let the 'weeds' actually choke the 'plants' as this would be a recipe for chaos!) Finally, they can mime the seeds that grow into big, healthy plants swaying in the wind, with arms held out to hold the 'heavy crops growing on our arms'. This type of active involvement will make a strong impression.

The senses

We can even involve the senses of taste and smell. When I tell the story of Jesus making breakfast for his disciples, I prepare a fire in the centre of the sandpit. We sit round the perimeter (outside the sandpit, for safety's sake) while the smell of fish fingers wafts from the fire. (I pre-cook these so that they will only need a few minutes on the fire to absorb a smoky flavour.) When the story is over, we share a 'breakfast' of fish fingers.

The auditory appeal of the story can be heightened by creating 'special effects' either with a tape recording or by using various implements. Two paper plates stapled together with dry peas or lentils between them makes a good noise for 'rain'. Try taping noises such as a crowd shouting or someone running. Be open to the leading of the Holy Spirit in thinking of different and exciting ways to bring stories alive by involving the senses.

STORY AIDS

The storyteller

The storyteller is the best story aid of all! God has equipped us fantastically as storytellers. We have bodies with which to make gestures, faces to contort into a hundred different expressions, and voices with a myriad of tonal variations!

When people say 'I can't tell stories!', my response is 'Can you use your voice?' If you can talk in a high or a low voice, if you can talk softly, loudly, quickly or slowly, then you can tell stories!

Imagine the scene you want to describe, and practice using a suitable voice. If you are a mouse, try talking in a high, squeaky voice. If you are a camel, what about a deep, slow voice? Think of the emotions of the characters. Use a fast, high voice to express fear or excitement. A slower pace will work if you want a sad, thoughtful or sleepy tone. Use a very loud voice, or a very soft one, for dramatic emphasis. A pause at the crucial moment greatly heightens a feeling of expectancy. The more you practice, the easier it becomes!

When using gestures in stories, overexaggerate: make 'larger than life' movements. Throw yourself totally into the story. When I am involved in drama, I find that to give my best I need to 'think myself' into the part I am playing. Last December we presented a play in which I took the part of a Yorkshire farmer witnessing the first Christmas. Afterwards, I couldn't have told you who was in the audience – I was completely absorbed in being 'Mr Llewellyn'. If I had allowed myself to think about those watching me at that moment, I wouldn't have been able to concentrate on the character I was playing.

Give your best to the children. Their natural affinity with the world of imagination makes them an appreciative audience!

Props

Many stories lend themselves to the use of a few simple props. For example, to tell the story of the woman who lost the coin (Luke 15:8-10), wrap a shawl around yourself and walk with a stoop. Repeatedly count out the ten silver coins, with the children's assistance. At the appropriate moment, let the shawl fall over one of the coins and slip it under a rug on the floor, without the children noticing (you hope). Then count the coins again, and find – there's one missing. Express concern and look frantically for it – until you find it under the mat!

For the story of Zacchaeus, put a small leafy branch in front of your face and look downwards when Zacchaeus is up in the tree. When Jesus is speaking, hold the branch above your head and look up into it. Simple props like these can be used to great effect.

Stories can also be illustrated with simple three-dimensional figures made of pipe-cleaners, corks, polystyrene or similar materials, with pieces of cloth wrapped around them for clothing. Place them in a sand-tray and move them appropriately as you tell the story.

Pictures

Pictures are an excellent visual aid in helping children to relate to the world of the Bible. For example, a camel is an animal which is likely to be unfamiliar to them, so a picture of one will help. Pictures must always be large enough to be seen clearly by every member of the group. It is best to have one picture to illustrate each key point of the story, numbered in order. You might find it helpful to write a few key words on the back of each, to remind you of the course of events. Hold the picture high enough for everyone to see, and only show the picture that relates directly to the part of the story being told, keeping the others out of sight. Colour your pictures with bold, realistic colour, and try to reflect the texture of what you are illustrating to add to the effect. (You may like to file the material for future use.)[1]

To get an idea of what I am suggesting, take a large piece of paper and a soft pencil. Try quickly sketching rain falling; water dripping from a tap; water running from a tap; water flowing over a waterfall; water squirting out from a circular water sprinkler; water in a still pond.

If this sounds intimidating, first go and observe some water. This will help you to see how the pencil strokes can naturally create different impressions. Observe textures. Close, even pencil strokes, flowing in the same direction, will capture the smooth surface of a wall. Follow the line of natural, waving textures to create the impression of cloth, hair or wool. Try looking at illustrations in books to see how artists gain effects.

Flannelgraph

This is often overlooked in favour of more 'glamorous' ways of displaying visual aids. However, in the hands of an expert, a flannelgraph can provide a riveting story experience. Pre-printed sets of flannelgraph pictures are available to buy, or you can make your own by drawing on thin card with cotton wool or small strips of sandpaper glued to the back. (These provide a surface that will remain stuck to the woolly surface of the flannelboard.)

Drawing directly on vilene (available in haberdashery departments) is very effective. Thin vilene will allow you to trace pictures you want to copy directly onto the fabric. Use felt-tipped pens or wax crayons to colour the pictures. If you use the latter, iron pictures between sheets of newspaper to set the wax. As before, ensure that each picture is large enough to be seen clearly by all the children.

Have the figures laid out in the order they are to be presented, and add each one as it is mentioned in the story. Remove those that are no longer relevant as you go. For example, for the story of Noah, once the animals have disembarked, replace the ark with the rainbow.

Store the sets of flannelgraph pictures, flat in clearly marked containers like shirt-boxes, for future use.

Puppets

There is something about puppets that immediately grabs children's attention. When you use them to tell a story, keep to a simple script with direct dialogue. Generally, aim for between two to five characters – too many will create confusion.

Puppets seem very real to young children, so the same puppet should always keep the same name and character (he can't be good Gordon today and naughty Sammy next week) and preferably always be portrayed by the same puppeteer. It's good to have more than one puppeteer for informal shows.

However many operators you have, you will need to use different voices to suit the different characters and the mood of the scene. Only move the character who is saying something – keep all the other puppets still. If all the puppets are moving, it isn't easy to identify which puppet is 'talking'.

Lip-synch is important with puppets that have 'talking mouths'. Practice using your puppet so that its mouth opens and closes in time with your speech, otherwise the show will be rather like a badly dubbed film.

Have the puppets ready in the order you plan to use them, and practice beforehand so that you can iron out any technical hitches. For example, one character may go off-stage and another puppet will have to be fitted onto the puppeteer's hand before that puppet can appear again; so the other puppeteer may have to 'chat' to the children or sing a short song using the puppet still on-stage to allow enough time for this change-over to happen. Sometimes I use a simple, well-known tune and make up a short song that relates to the story. The puppet sings this at appropriate times throughout the show, encouraging the children to join in. For example, if I am doing a nativity playlet, 'Mary' may sing, to the tune of 'Mary had a little lamb':

Jesus is the baby's name,
>   baby's name, baby's name.
Jesus is the baby's name,
>   God's special baby boy.'

You want to hold the children's attention for the duration of the show. Ask someone else to watch you practice and give feedback, as it's difficult to assess the effect from behind the stage. Particular things you may need to watch include the following:

- Puppets should be held so they are facing the audience.

- If two puppets are having a 'conversation', ensure that they face each other at an angle of 45 degrees. Their faces will still be clearly visible to the audience, but it will seem as though the puppets are looking at each other.

- Hold puppets at the correct height. If they are held too high, the operator's arm will show; if too low, the puppet's face will only be partially visible.

- The puppet's head should be in an upright natural position, unless he is 'crying' or 'sleeping'. Don't let the head droop forward or flop backwards so that the face isn't visible.

- Avoid 'dead puppet syndrome'. At all times, hold the puppet in a position that gives the impression he is 'alive' and 'listening' to the conversation of the other puppets.

- Puppets should 'walk' horizontally off-stage (when you are using a puppet-theatre with curtains). Avoid the impression that the puppet has dropped through a hole in the ground.

Over the years I have collected an array of beautiful puppets, but most characters can be made out of simple scraps. Once I bought an expensive fish puppet for a particular story I was presenting. A week later I found a stimulating book on puppetry with a wealth of ideas for home-made puppets. It gave directions for a fish puppet made with a clothes-peg and two paper plates, which would have worked equally well. The book cost only double the amount that the one puppet had cost me, and has given me ideas for many inexpensive but effective puppets. I have created a basic animal puppet which has small Velcro strips sewn in position for the features. I use an array of noses and pairs of ears and eyes to change the puppet into different characters. If I need a donkey, I add long upright ears and a flat broad nose. If I need a mouse, I add small rounded ears and a small triangular nose. I could use the same concept to make a 'human' puppet by changing eyebrows, hair colour and style, mouth expression and other features. A basic puppet can be used to create a myriad of characters.[2]

Young children may be frightened by large unfamiliar creatures, so when working with the under sixes choose small, friendly puppets that the children will feel comfortable with (such as mice and rabbits). Smaller puppets such as glove- or finger-puppets work well. Leave larger characters for older children.

Children love to interact with the puppets during the performance, but be careful to have closed questions that encourage one-word (or very short) responses — it is more difficult to control the children when you are out of sight! Don't ask things like 'What did you have for breakfast today?' or 'What is your favourite colour?' Every child would be shouting a different answer. Ask questions like 'What day is it today?' or 'Did you see my friend? Which way did he go?' (when the puppet is 'looking for' the other puppet who has just exited).

Puppets can easily be used to evoke humour or relieve stress. A puppet-play showing the consequences of aggressive or negative patterns of behaviour can be useful for teaching positive ways of handling difficult situations without having to reprimand a child directly. For example, if a child is repeatedly taking things that belong to others, a puppet story depicting a similar situation might strike a chord with her. The other puppets could cry and say that they feel sad because their toys are missing. The 'naughty' puppet then tells the children that *he* feels bad because his friends are sad. In his interaction with the children, he might ask, 'Should I say sorry?' or 'Look, I've got Jane's sweet? Shall I hide it away? What shall I do with it?'

Children have a natural sense of justice which will be called into play when you give them the opportunity to call out a solution. But be careful not to make the message too pointed, otherwise the child concerned may feel embarrassed and reject the puppet's message. *Never* give the puppets the same names as the children in your group.

Puppets are great fun, but have a clear objective when you are using them. The children should remember the story rather than the puppets!

LETTING A STORY SPEAK FOR ITSELF

Don't 'kill' a story by explaining its meaning to the children: rather, let it 'speak for itself'. Jesus used parables as an illustration of God's kingdom; but in nearly all cases he left it to us to figure out the deeper meaning for ourselves. Trust God that, as we faithfully lay the foundations, *he* will build on them in his own good time. Our job is to leave children with the warm, satisfying feeling of having enjoyed a good story.

Notes

1 Scripture Union SALT resources provide clear illustrations for group work, often with black-and-white outlines to cut printing costs and keep the material readily affordable. *How to Cheat at Visual Aids!* and *How to Cheat at Visual Aids – Old Testament* (by Judith Merrell and Pauline Adams) are two good sources of artwork and ideas to help create your own visual aids.

2 Two good books are Fran Rottman's *Easy-to-make Puppets and How to Use Them* (Book 1), *Early Childhood* (Book 2), Children/Youth, 1978 (fourth printing 1984), Regal Books (US).

Chapter 8

Encouraging creativity

'Choose whatever colours you like,' I instructed, 'and paint how you are feeling today.'

Most children splashed away happily with bright, cheerful colours. Roger took the pot of black paint and deliberately smothered the entire surface of his paper, even obliterating his name which had been written in the corner.

'How are you feeling today?' I enquired gently, kneeling next to him.

'Bad,' he thundered, not even looking up from his stormy paper.

Creative activities often provide a natural release for pent-up emotions, particularly for young children whose vocabulary is not yet adequate to express how they feel. In fact, the area of creativity is perhaps one in which the physical, cognitive, socio-emotional and spiritual aspects are all nurtured. The child's self-knowledge and observation skills are sharpened. His fine-muscle control is exercised. He can interact with his peers while he works, especially as he grows older.

God said, 'Let us create man in our own image' (Gen 1:26). Part of God's image is his creative nature. Within each one of us is a desire to create. This may be expressed in a number of ways – through drawing, designing, gardening, dressmaking, painting, making models, problem-solving, and so on. All these creative activities have certain characteristics in common. They give us the opportunity to open our souls, to experience the wonder of creation and of being creative. The word in the

Afrikaans language for 'open' is 'oop' (pronounced *oo-wp*). 'Oop' forms an acrostic: Ownership, Originality, Process. When we prepare any form of creative activity, we can use this acrostic as a guide. Let's consider the three characteristics.

Ownership

When she has finished what she is making, a child might comment, 'I made it myself'. She has to 'own' her creation. If a task is too difficult, she is deprived of personal satisfaction.

Originality

Creativity is original, and every picture is different. At no time should the adult draw or paint an example for children to copy. This will inhibit their natural gift of self-expression.

Process

The process of creation is more important than the product. The child's hands-on experience matters more than the quality of the final product. Too often we become 'parent pleasers', sending home some near-perfect object which has basically been made by the teacher. It is far more significant for children to be absorbed in the process, even if the end-product leaves much to be desired in the adult's eyes. A child who has splodged red paint unrecognisably over the paper has been involved in the process. If the leader draws the 'perfect picture' instead of allowing the child to make her own attempts, the child's experiential learning is being hampered.

> It has been proved beyond any doubt that such imitative procedures as found in colouring books and workbooks make the child dependent in his thinking; they make the child inflexible because he has to follow what he has been given. They do not provide emotional relief because they give the child no opportunity to express his own emotions; they do not even promote skills and discipline, because the child's urge for perfection grows out of his urge for expression; and finally, they condition the child to adult concepts

which he cannot produce alone, and which therefore frustrate his own creative ambitions.[1]

THE GOALS OF CREATIVE ACTIVITIES

In my introduction to this book, we considered our goal in working with young children, which is to guide them to responsible adulthood. As we reflect on the qualities required by the young adult to meet the challenges of the twenty-first century, the importance of developing creativity cannot be overemphasised.

Our goals in creative activities include:

- Giving children the opportunity for emotional relief, so that they learn how to cope with their emotions.

- Giving children the opportunity for self-expression.

- Giving them the opportunity to experience different media and to use different equipment.

- Promoting the skills used in creativity.

- Building children's confidence in their own abilities.

- Developing an appreciation of beauty.

- Developing lateral thinking and problem-solving skills.

To sum up, our aim is to provide children with an equipped environment that encourages them to take part in stimulating art activities. As guides, we want them to experiment with new media and techniques, and to develop their skills of observation.[2]

COMMENTING ON CREATIVE WORK

Praise children's efforts and display their work, but avoid giving 'prizes' such as stickers as a reward. Children, like adults, enjoy the experience of personal satisfaction in a job well done. They need our affirmation, so be sincere in complimenting their efforts. A good way to start is to say 'Tell me about your picture' (which sounds far more diplomatic than 'What on earth is this?'). This gives them the opportunity to verbalise what they are trying to express. My son once brought home a picture from nursery school, which at first I couldn't figure out. In the centre was a blue circle within a yellow square. The background was coloured totally orange. 'Tell me about your picture,' I prompted. He explained that it was Mummy's new tumble-drier. Suddenly his strange picture took on meaning: the circular door within the square frame of the tumble-drier standing on the ochre-coloured floor of my kitchen.

Take time to study each child's picture and make appropriate, sincere comments. You could say, 'I like your colours' or 'You drew your people carefully' or 'You worked hard today'. Avoid gushing comments such as 'Beautiful!' Children quickly sense insincerity. It is important to understand and accept their art at each stage of their development. They must feel confident that every effort is valued as an achievement. This will motivate them to continue trying. When we chat to children about their pictures and display them, we are indicating that we value their work. Pictures thrown into the dustbin give the message, 'This is rubbish!'

Children who have already developed the basic skills of working with drawing, painting, cutting and modelling materials are usually confident enough to receive comments that will help them improve. If a child brings me a competently drawn picture with features, hands and fingers – but has left the body with no clothing – I might ask, 'Isn't she going to get cold without any clothes on?' If a four- or five-year-old brings a nicely drawn picture without arms, I might comment, 'But how will she eat her food?' This type of response appeals to children's sense of humour and spurs them on to do their best.

Encourage children to observe the object or creature they want to draw carefully. For example, if a child says he doesn't know how to draw arms, you could take him to a full-length mirror and discuss what you both see.

'Show me your arms.'

'Which part of your body do they come from?'

'What do they look like?'
'Do any parts of your arms bend?'
'What is at the end of your arm?'

Look at trees, leaves, clouds, people, animals. Bring flowers, plants, creatures, pieces of driftwood, all sorts of things for the children to observe and draw!

Commenting on children's art requires great sensitivity. Get to know individual children in your group, their abilities, emotional state and level of confidence. Children lacking in confidence may need wholehearted approval of their pictures just as they are, whereas children who are established in the group and coping well may thrive on the stimulation of being challenged to look more closely and draw in more detail. I have been surprised this year to discover how well even the four-year-old group in my care can express themselves through art when they are given guidance and sufficient stimulation.

We have a responsibility to encourage parents to adopt a positive attitude towards their children's work: parental encouragement will foster children's belief in their own ability. It is recognised that the greater children's self-confidence, the more they will be prepared to take risks and try out new ideas – qualities which are evident in all achievers.

PLANNING ACTIVITIES

When beginning to work with a new group of young children, start with the simplest materials and equipment, and then gradually increase the challenge. To nurture the children's creativity, provide a variety of activities – drawing, painting, three-dimensional modelling, and cutting and pasting. Like adults, not every child enjoys the same sort of activity and it is important to have a choice available. A child will apply himself better to a task he wants to do, and he learns to make independent decisions when he has to make choices. Remember, a good rule is to have the same number of activities as the age of the child, up to a maximum of six (ie with the three-year-olds provide three activities such as painting, drawing and a three-dimensional activity).

Remember too to organise your environment so as to encourage children to do things for themselves and not to 'wait for the teacher' (see chapter five).

Getting ready

Prior to the session, prepare art materials so that children can begin working immediately. Plan to have one adult-directed activity related to the theme of the session and requiring a fairly high level of interaction with the children. The activity might involve the children mastering a new skill. Any other activities should be a free choice and simple enough for the children to work on independently.

Begin by briefly explaining the activities available to the children. Ask them, 'Who would like to go and play with the dough?' Some children will want to do this and will move to that activity.

'Who would like to draw a picture?' More children will volunteer for this.

The remaining group is likely to be small enough to tackle the leader-directed activity. If there are still a few too many children, some could read a book or play with blocks until you are ready for them. Assure them that they will each have a turn, and make sure you keep your promise!

Drawing

At first young children are intrigued to discover that drawing implements make marks on paper. They enjoy the experience, even though their efforts look meaningless to the casual observer (the 'scribble stage'). As they become more familiar with creating their own lines, their scribbles become more controlled and begin to have names. If you say to a child 'Tell me about your picture', she may say 'This is me' even though 'me' is unrecognisable.

This stage usually lasts to about the age of three or four. However, if children haven't had previous exposure to creative materials, they are likely to begin at the scribble stage, even if they are six or seven. Their scribbles will quickly become recognisable pictures.

Later, children begin to draw shapes, combining lines and circles to create simple figures. Three- to four-year-olds may draw a 'potato man', with legs coming directly off a circular shape. The circle represents the whole body, and they tend to place facial features fairly centrally within it. Eventually they add arms and then a head distinguishable from the body.

Thick wax crayons and pastels are an ideal medium for pre-schoolers, who enjoy bold colour that they can apply easily. Children under the age of six need implements that have a broad surface for them to grip. Charcoal, chalk and broad felt-tips are also good. Ordinary pencil-crayons, fine felt-tips and pencils are best kept for the over-sixes.

Use different textured, coloured and shaped papers to add interest – perhaps even newspaper, paper plates and blocks of wood that the children have sanded. Occasionally cut the paper in an unusual shape. For instance, when telling the story of the feeding of the five thousand, I provide circular pieces of paper (to represent baskets) and encourage the children to draw the loaves and fish. Children are interested in texture and enjoy taking rubbings from different surfaces. The soles of running shoes make very interesting prints, and the children have fun trying to identify whose shoes made which prints! (Remember, the younger the child the larger the paper – a minimum size of A3 for three-year-olds.)

Paint and paper

When a new group commences, even the simplest activity has to be learned. A three-year-old enthusiastically wielding a paint-laden brush can have horrific consequences! We need to think about how to train children in the necessary skills.

For example, in showing children how to use paint, make sure the paint is pre-mixed and in spill-proof tubs. Provide brushes in each colour. An effective paint-pot stand can be made by standing yogurt tubs in an up-ended plastic two-litre ice-cream tub, in which suitable holes have been cut for the pots. Paint the tip of each brush-handle the same colour as the paint in which it will be used. Demonstrate the steps thus:

'The red brush goes in the red paint. I lift the brush and go wipe, wipe on the side of the pot' (to remove excess paint).

'Then I lift the brush carefully to the paper and paint. When I have finished painting, the red brush goes back in the red paint.'

This is a major learning task for a three-year-old and he will need constant supervision for the first few times!

Powder paints, or similar pre-mixed colours that are bold and easy to apply, are the most satisfying for young children. Two or three colours are adequate for the three-year-old; provide more for older children. Mix colours that are appropriate to your theme. For example, if you are talking about autumn, provide shades of yellow, brown and orange. If you are talking about summer, provide bright, bold colours. If you are talking about a story with animals, provide suitable browns, yellows and blacks to paint the creatures.

By the age of six, children are ready to mix their own colours. Introduce this as a learning experience, giving them the opportunity to work initially with only two primary colours at a time plus white; then extend the range to blue, red, yellow and white, to see all the different colours and shades they can make. Provide a good quality brush, a container of clean water, a piece of sponge (to wipe the brush clean after rinsing in water), an ozone-friendly polystyrene tray (or white plastic lid) on which to mix colours, powder paint with a plastic teaspoon in each colour, and paper.

Encourage children to create their own colours by experimenting, but first teach the technique of mixing colours and then cleaning the brush before making a new colour. For example, spoon a small quantity of red and yellow paint onto the polystyrene tray. Use the brush to mix the colours with a small quantity of water and then apply the colour to the paper. Add more of either colour or white to create a new shade. For a first colour-mixing activity, I encourage children to paint small circles of each new colour, without being concerned about producing a picture. Once the children are confident about mixing colours, they will enjoy creating their own paintings. A variety of painting implements and techniques can be introduced, such as finger-painting, making handprints and footprints, and using cotton-buds and different sized paintbrushes.

Use aprons when you are finger-painting, as this is messy. Add pre-cooked starch to the paint, and work on a waterproof table-top, creating pictures directly in the paint. Give two dollops of different primary colours for a colour-mixing experience. Older children could work individually, using a discarded X-ray sheet or firm plastic sheet as a base. Try drawing a picture directly into the finger-paint and then smoothing a piece of paper over the surface to make a print of the design. If you decide to make handprints or footprints, have bowls of warm, soapy water for cleaning up operations!

Printing activities add great variety to painting. Possibilities include:

- Cutting potatoes, or sections of other fruit and vegetables, into shapes, dipping the cut-side of a shape into paint and using it to make a series of prints. Shapes can also be cut out of sponge, Duplo blocks, cotton reels or polystyrene blocks.

- Rolling marbles into paint and then onto paper inside a shirt-box. Do this with older children only; younger ones might swallow the marbles!

- Wheeling toy cars through a thin layer of paint and then onto paper, creating tyre tracks.

- Making prints out of prepared wooden printing blocks onto which pieces of pipe-cleaner have been arranged and glued. Older children can make these themselves.

To get the best paint consistency for printing, pour thin pre-mixed paint onto shallow blocks of sponge in shallow containers, such as two-litre plastic ice-cream tubs. Place the printing block on the sponge and then press it onto the paper. This will give a good, even layer of paint.

Three-dimensional modelling

Children like the relaxation of three-dimensional modelling. Playdough in particular has a therapeutic effect. A colleague of mine worked in a nursery school which was attached to a children's home. Many of the children were emotionally disturbed. At any time of day, the playdough table would always have children sitting deeply engrossed as they pulled and pushed the dough to express their pent-up frustration and pain.

Playdough is comforting: whatever you make is acceptable, and if you don't like it you can bash it down and start again! Playdough is a particularly good medium for very young children and for any who are new to your group. It can be bought readily from educational distributors and lasts for weeks, provided it is sealed in an air-tight container when not in use. Home-made playdough is also good, but you will need to ensure that it is sufficiently malleable and doesn't crumble when handled.

Children enjoy moulding the dough with their hands, but provide different equipment to stimulate their play, such as ice-lolly sticks, rollers (plastic ones can be purchased or wooden ones made by cutting short lengths from a wooden broomstick), plastic bottle-tops, dough-cutters, plastic animals and plastic knives.

Salt dough is made by mixing equal parts of salt and flour, with enough water for a firm consistency. When left in the sun this dries hard, so it is ideal for making small models or beads, which can be painted a few days later.

Another form of three-dimensional work is box construction. Provide a variety of small cardboard cartons – jelly- and medicine-boxes, egg-boxes, toilet-roll centres, scissors, glue and brushes. Leave the children free to create. Masking tape is good for joining things, but short strips of firm paper, which the child glues, work well for taping 3-D constructions together.

Both boys and girls enjoy sewing. Provide large, blunt tapestry needles double-threaded with wool, and they can make necklaces by stringing together circular-shaped breakfast cereals, daisies, polystyrene chips or short pre-cut lengths of coloured plastic drinking straws. Older children can add buttons, sequins, lace and other small scraps of fabric to their sewing creations. They could also use sections of nylon net-bags like those in which oranges and vegetables are sometimes purchased. (Staple a small rectangle of the net onto a pre-cut cardboard frame.) Using a needle to push a pattern of holes into a cardboard frame or polystyrene tray is fun!

Woodwork

Woodwork is another great stress reliever, provided there is enough space to absorb the noise. Sanding wood, hammering nails, drilling holes, screwing in screws, and sawing wood give children the satisfaction of feeling that they are doing 'grown-up' work, as well as improving their motor skills. If possible, provide a wooden, child-height workbench fitted with one or two small vices, small fretsaws with fine-toothed blades, sandpaper, a few round-headed hammers, a hand-drill, nails and screws. Buy good quality tools that are meant to be used, not cheap imitations which will only lead to frustration. Always ensure that an adult closely supervises this activity, teaching each child how to handle the tools correctly. Provide scraps of soft wood, and look out for other interesting oddments, such as bottle-tops and leather off-cuts, which the children can add to their creations.

Cutting and pasting

Cutting is something that children will master as their fine-motor skills improve. Supply pairs of good quality, blunt-nosed scissors (sharp points can be dangerous), as well as left-handed scissors and training scissors (which adult and child operate together). Small pairs of scissors that create a zig-zag edge are fun to use when children have become more competent.

Activities that will help very young children to improve fine-motor skills include:

- Tearing, crumpling and gluing small pieces of soft paper (eg tissue paper, newspaper, coloured 'sugar paper').

- Snipping thin card.
- Cutting playdough.
- Cutting 'in the air'.
- Cutting on a broad straight line (progressing later to wavy lines, large circles and then angular lines).

To teach a child how to use a pair of scissors, the leader first needs to help him hold the scissors properly and show him how to guide the paper. When the child can hold the scissors comfortably and make random 'snips', I find it helpful to pretend that the two blades of the scissors are like a crocodile's mouth, opening and closing. (Draw a set of eyes on the top blade of the scissors with a thin black marker pen.) Using a piece of paper with a broad, curving line drawn on it, show the child that the cut will come where the crocodile looks at the line. If the crocodile doesn't keep looking at the line, he won't cut on the line. This helps the child learn how to direct the scissors.

When they have mastered cutting straight lines, children can progress to curved and later to angular lines. For the latter, show them how to cut right up to the apex of the angle, stop, realign the scissors and then cut again. By the age of four, a child can cope with cutting most shapes if he has been taught the skills.

Cutting pictures from old gift wrap, greeting cards and magazines is a popular activity. When using magazines, tear out suitable pictures beforehand, which relate to the theme (rather than just providing a pile of magazines from which the children indiscriminately tear pages).

Children like drawing or painting their own pictures and cutting them out. This develops their cutting skills and is very satisfying. With a subject such as Noah's ark, some children might help to paint a large ark on background paper, while others choose what animals to draw, colour their pictures, cut them out and then paste them onto the ark.

Collage is a particularly enjoyable creative activity for young children. Collect all sorts of household junk, such as toilet-roll

centres, buttons, scraps of fabric, lace, sequins, wool, and so on. Try to obtain old wallpaper catalogues. Make a collage tray with six to eight compartments, and provide materials that fit in with your theme. For example, if the children are going to be creating animals, choose natural coloured wool, leather off-cuts, fabric scraps, ice-lolly sticks, halved sections of toilet rolls, and buttons. Before you begin, show the children the materials one by one, and let them suggest what each could be used for. Have ample pairs of scissors and pots of glue (PVA or acrylic glue would be most suitable). Provide firm card for the children to work on, such as pre-cut sections from cereal boxes.

Collage can also be used in making models (cardboard wine-bottle sleeves make a good base), paper-bag puppets and masks (using thin card or paper plates). Encourage older children to use their puppets or models to enact a story. For example, if they have chosen to make the different characters of the nativity scene, they could prepare a simple playlet to put on for parents.

Combining media

Encourage children to experiment by combining different art media. For example, to create an underwater picture, they might use oil pastels and a wash of blue food colouring; to make night pictures, white wax-crayon stars overlaid with a black wash. Or a child might paint a countryside scene, then choose to draw and cut out animals to paste onto it. He might draw a person, choose pieces of fabric to paste on for clothes, and then paint in a background.

SPECIAL SEASONAL PICTURES

Many of us who happily plan exciting activities for most weeks of the year get stuck when it comes to Christmas and Easter. Then we revert to handing out photocopies of, say, an adult's impression of an angel, and asking the children to colour and cut out! Although there is a place for teaching skills such as making paper-chains or other Christmas decorations, keep looking for opportunities to encourage the children to be creative.

The marble-rolling technique already described, using two different shades of green paint, makes an attractive, leafy 'Christmas tree' which the children can then cut out and add to their own 'Christmas decorations'. Three-dimensional and/or collage materials can be provided for them to create a nativity scene. When preparing a collage tray for the children to use to make angels, I set out sections of small doilies, small flesh-coloured ovals, pre-cut strands of natural coloured wool, gold and silver foil paper, small strips of tinsel and glitter. Every year I am delighted at the beautiful angels the children create without any adult intervention!

DISPLAYING CHILDREN'S ART

Mount children's pictures on the walls at their eye level – it is they who most want to see their work! If you have the permanent use of a room, create a space for each child, with a large, clear name label so that he knows that this is where his work will be placed. If a child isn't yet able to write his own name, do it for him in the top left-hand corner of his piece of artwork, in lower-case lettering of the style he will be taught when he goes to school. (This encourages reading skills – we read from top left to bottom right.) Write the title of the picture in the top centre of the paper.

As in an art gallery, display pictures with enough space around them to give a clean, uncluttered look. Approximately one-third of the wall space should be left blank so as to balance the busy areas. Encourage children to decide which pictures they should put on the wall. At any time, I have a variety of different themes displayed as each child decides when she wishes to put up a new picture in place of an old one.

CONCLUSION

Art may be described as autobiographical, an expression of oneself. In art, we not only provide opportunities for the development of skills, but also give children the chance to express themselves, building their self-esteem as we accept and commend their personal statements. Piaget declared that the principle goal of education is 'to create (people) who are capable of doing new things, not simply of repeating what other generations have done, (people) who are creative, inventive and discoverers'. What a challenge!

Notes

1   J Isenberg and M Jolongo, *Creative Expression and Play in the Early Childhood Curriculum*, Macmillan Publishing Company (US), 1993; emphasising a statement by Viktor Lowenfeld.

2   A recommended book for doing art with children is: Peggy D Jenkins, *Art for the Fun of it: A Guide for Teaching Young Children*, Spectrum Books (US), 1980.

Chapter 9

Dealing with discipline

In considering the issue of discipline, let's look again at the 'big picture'. What are we actually trying to achieve, as parents, leaders or teachers? At the beginning of this book we focused on the main goal (as outlined by Dr Luke) which was to help children grow wise and strong, to please God and to learn to live peacefully with others (Luke 2:52). God has given the responsibility of wise instruction to us, children's caregivers (Prov 1:8). We have to provide a safe and secure environment for them to grow in. Children please God as they learn moral standards, develop spiritual maturity and gain an understanding of him. They can live at peace with others when they learn how to control their own emotions and how to treat those around them with respect. In doing so, they develop an understanding of how much they need other people.

Discipline plays an important part in the nurture of all aspects of a child's development. Just as a young plant needs a suitable climate in order to grow healthily, so does a child. He requires an ordered programme, a settled environment and consistent handling. And just as someone running a garden-centre needs to know how to care for plants, so we need to know how to care for children. A nurseryman wouldn't want to leave his plants in the hands of an uninformed attendant: plants which are left wilting without water, or which are pruned unthinkingly, may suffer permanent damage. Likewise, parents have entrusted their children to us; and we need to recognise that our handling of a child at this tender stage can enhance or damage his growth.

Our methods of discipline should be directly linked to our goal of helping children become responsible adults. Nurturing children is a process that takes patience and time. We live in an 'instant' world – instant coffee, instant cereal, even travel is close on 'instant' (sometimes!). We can become so used to this that we expect instant solutions to human relationships too.

I sometimes hear parents sigh, 'It's a pity children don't come with an instruction manual.' I challenge that children do come with such a manual, but many of us forget to refer to it! The Bible offers us some sound principles on child-raising, which we can relate to the everyday situations we encounter. But the Bible's advice on child-raising isn't neatly arranged on a few pages and clearly headed 'How to raise children'. We need to take time to study God's word in order to know his way. If you want to start developing a Bible-reading routine, why not try reading one chapter of Proverbs on each day of the month? (There are thirty-one chapters.) Each day, make a note of at least one verse that has particular meaning for you. Place it on the fridge or somewhere you will be reminded of it. In my own journal, a verse that has been significant to me is Proverbs 4:3 which begins, 'When I was a boy learning from my father, when I was still tender and an only child of my mother…' I underlined one word – 'tender' – and spent time reflecting on it:

> *A young plant has tender shoots: they are still forming; they can be easily harmed; rough handling can cause permanent damage; they need careful and gentle nurturing.*

Such meditative reading of even one word can increase our understanding.

If our goal is to raise loving, caring people, then we need to consider whether our methods of discipline are likely to achieve this. Far too often we raise our voices to relieve pent-up frustrations without any thought about the possible long-term effect upon the child. 'While threatening measures may temporarily solve an immediate problem for a teacher, in no way do they improve children's behaviour. On the contrary, they are a model of how to be an angry, yelling person who humiliates others' (Claire Cherry). It is always good to put yourself in the child's shoes. Would *you* like someone perpetually yelling at you, especially in front of other people? The Bible tells us to treat our children with sensitivity and respect (Col 3:21). It seems more sensible to create an environment where children are taught self-control by the example adults are setting.

THE LEADER'S EXAMPLE

I love to tell the story of Mr and Mrs Measles who decided that they wanted their children to be different from themselves. They thought it would be better for their offspring to have mumps. So Mr and Mrs Measles carefully explained all about mumps. They found pictures in books of what mumps looked like. They did all they could to teach their children about mumps. But you can guess what their children soon had – measles, just like their parents! Behaviour is more often caught than taught, and children will learn more about God's love through how we treat them than through what we say.

I write this knowing full well that I am *not* the perfect model. No doubt, my own sons would be the first to affirm that! However, over the years I have become more and more convinced that our methods of discipline need to be an integral part of our attitude to child-raising. The word 'discipline' stems from the word 'disciple' which means 'to guide', and this is surely affirmation of our overall goal as carers. Children who know they are respected will feel confident, and confident children are prepared to take risks and to explore their surroundings. Children learn through activity, through doing! Confident children will do more, and children who do more will learn more!

> Because our world is filled with uncertainty, even under the most ideal circumstances, children are prone to self-doubt. Our goals should be to promote the children's active independence, self-confidence, and awareness of their own capabilities. We need to think in terms of

> raising courageous young people who can face the vigorous challenges of a rapidly changing society. Through encouragement we can help children learn to surmount their problems. We can acknowledge the difficulty of a situation and help them learn that, through perseverance, industriousness, and practice, they can overcome obstacles.[1]

I once heard a mother say that she used to pray for God to change her children, but over the years her prayer changed to 'God, please change me'. Children are astute observers and are well aware if our walk doesn't match our talk. They learn from our example. Can we say, with Paul, 'You know the teachings I gave you, and you know what you heard me say and saw me do. So follow my example' (Phil 4:9)?

The child, like each one of us, needs an atmosphere of acceptance, unconditional love and security, and it is the leader who creates this. Treat every child with the courtesy you would expect. 'What I want for myself, I must also want for you; what I want from you, I must always be willing to give' (Cherry). Every child needs to know that the adults who care for him will always be consistent, caring and fair in their dealings with him. None of us is perfect – and we all occasionally lose our cool – but if you do 'blow it', apologise. Children are forgiving and are happy to know that adults are human too! Our humility in saying sorry sets an example.

Children are great readers of body language and are perceptive to the tone of our voices. Create a calm, loving atmosphere by speaking and moving in a calm, loving manner. Listen with your body as well as your ears; keep your body language open, attentive and focused on the child. Trust breeds trust. Treat a child's comments with the same confidentiality you would an adult's. Concentrate on the child and his needs. Our time with children is not the time to chat to our colleagues or to parents. When I greet my nursery school class, I immediately drop down to their eye-level so that they know I am 'there for them'.

A student teacher once said to me, 'When I get to the school gate I stop and put down my bag of troubles. I only pick them up again when I walk out of the gate to go home.'

Instilling respect

We live in a world where care and respect for people are often absent. In a recent comedy television show, a toddler was asked, 'What's Daddy's other name?'

The child immediately responded, 'Moron.'

Funny? When we undermine authority in the home, the child is left with nothing else to build on.

We can't change home situations, but we can set children the example of respect and caring for one another while they are with us.

Give instructions simply

Recently I chatted with my class about not sitting on furniture unless it was made for that purpose. Shortly afterwards, a three-year-old was perched on the table again.

'Luke,' I reprimanded him, 'didn't Auntie Val ask you *not* to sit on the furniture?'

He gave me his endearing smile. 'That's not furniture,' he said. 'That's a *table!*'

What is obvious to an adult isn't necessarily obvious to a pre-schooler. Sometimes children don't follow instructions because they don't understand what is required of them. We can bombard them with too much language, so that they eventually just 'tune out'.

Listen to yourself. Are you talking too much and too quickly? Use words children understand. Talk clearly, audibly and not too fast. Use short sentences. Give specific instructions when you want children to do something. Say a child's name first, to get his attention (eg 'Brendan, please sit down *now*').

Encourage co-operation

Sometimes children's lack of co-operation is triggered by adult insensitivity. One thing that really made me mad as a child was when adults didn't say 'Please' or 'Thank you'. Treat children with courtesy whenever you ask them to do something. And don't interrupt them. If a child is engrossed in a task, warn him at least five minutes in advance that it will soon be time to pack away. If a child has nearly finished a drawing or building a jigsaw puzzle, give him enough time to complete the task. This may mean the rest of the group starts on something else.

If children aren't enthusiastic about packing up, work alongside them. Be specific when you delegate tasks. Don't just say, 'Everyone pack away' – everyone will wait for someone else to do it! Rather, encourage the children to pack up in the areas they are working.

'John and Ann, please pick the papers off the floor.'

'Ursula, please put the crayons away.'

Each child then knows what is expected. And praise children for tasks willingly completed.

Involving children in the clearing up helps them to learn to be responsible and considerate of others. They will be encouraged to take a pride in the appearance of the room as they pack up equipment they have used and throw scraps in the dustbin. Even a simple task, such as quietly pushing a chair in, is a useful skill for a young child to learn.

REINFORCING POSITIVE BEHAVIOUR

When my older son was a baby he had what his grandmother called a 'naughty finger'. When he was told 'No' he would advance, his digit finger creeping closer and closer to the forbidden 'fruit', whilst his eyes remained fixed on the reprimanding adult. It seemed he just had to find out if we really meant what we said! (Of course, there are times, such as when a child wishes to investigate an electric socket, that 'No' is 'No' and there can be no negotiation.) Not every child is going to be a model child, even if we strive to be model leaders. 'A child will kick until he feels the walls.' He needs to know what behaviour is acceptable and what isn't, and he discovers this by pushing against the boundaries.

Make as few rules as possible

Don't have too many rules: children will never remember them all. KIS (keep it simple)! Try to ensure that the environment is as child-proof as possible, and then work out which rules are absolutely necessary for the safety and welfare of all group members: so 'Please walk in this room' (ie 'Don't run') helps prevent accidents.

Discuss rules with the children, encouraging them to say why each is important. 'No screaming unless you are hurt' is one I insist on. Some children scream in excitement, but I want to know when a child's scream means he needs my immediate response. 'Young children are more apt to take ownership of their behaviour when they hear themselves verbalise the rules and receive praise for the right answers' (Ezzo).[2]

Be consistent but flexible

Have as few rules as possible, but make sure the children know that those rules stand. If we aren't consistent, they won't feel secure.

However, we need to be flexible too: we may have to bend a rule on a particular occasion. If so, explain to the children that this is only for this one specific time. Perhaps children aren't usually allowed to ride tricycles in the corridors, but on a very rainy day I may make an exception. I explain that we may ride tricycles in the corridor *just for today*.

Mean what you say

Avoid threats as far as possible, and always mean what you say. Recently we had supper at a restaurant with friends. The six-year-old was toying with his food. His exasperated father said, 'If you don't eat your supper, I'm leaving you here tonight.'

Children aren't stupid. They know when threats won't be carried out!

When Jamie throws sand in the other children's eyes, I firmly tell him 'No' and explain that this will hurt the others. If he does it again, I repeat 'No' and tell him that if he carries on behaving like that, he may not play in the sandpit. If a third incident occurs, I remove him from the play-area.

Let the punishment fit the crime

As far as possible, choose a form of punishment that relates to the crime. Disciplinary action doesn't need to be lengthy. Very often for three-year-old Jamie, a ten-minute break from the sandpit will be sufficient for him to realise that this behaviour isn't acceptable. I always ensure that the offender says sorry to God and the other people involved before he can resume play.

Children's body language is usually a good indicator of their mood. A prolonged punishment or a delayed one can be unbearably agonising, so act immediately and keep punishments short. Always assure children that you still love them, even though you are unhappy with their actions. When 'making up' after an upset, I always give children a hug, just to reassure them that they are still precious.

Let children face the consequences of their actions

I once heard a minister preach that one of the greatest mistakes of this generation is not allowing our children to face the consequences of their actions. Perhaps our busy lifestyle – the juggling of home, family and often work too – instils this over-concern within us. But we do our children a disservice.

Peter is told, 'Put your lunchbox in your bag.' After he has gone to school Mum finds the lunchbox standing on the kitchen table. Wanting to be a 'good mother', she jumps in the car and delivers the lunchbox. I'm guilty of doing things like this. I can't bear to think of my 'starving' child. But the child who misses his lunch-time snack today will be more careful to remember his mother's instructions in future.

Obviously young children can't adequately anticipate danger, and we have to protect them from harmful situations. However, there are many other areas in which we can teach them to take responsibility for themselves.

Word instructions positively

Verbs ('doing' words) are words children relate to far more readily than other parts of speech. When you say 'Don't run!', a child doesn't hear 'Don't' – he hears 'Run'. A negative command is likely to reinforce the very behaviour you wish to stop. So rephrase the command. Instead of saying 'Don't run', say 'Walk'. Instead of saying 'Don't walk on the grass', say 'Walk on the path'.

Criticise or praise the action, not the person

We all thrive on praise, so give it generously – but always sincerely. The leader who enthuses 'Beautiful' at every picture she is shown will soon have a group of demotivated children. The unexpected word of praise is the most meaningful of all. Often we notice the very good children and the very naughty children, and somehow there are always a few in the middle who just 'blend in'. Often it's these children who are most in need of a compliment.

Always comment on a child's action and not on the child himself. Say 'That was a kind thing to do' rather than 'You're an angel'. He won't be able to live up to an unrealistic image of himself. When reprimanding, I don't say 'You were a bad boy', but 'That was a bad thing to do'.

Allow time to 'cool off'

Often children don't know how to express their feelings. Our culture often discourages boys from giving vent to 'soft' emotions, so they tend to bottle these up instead. Children often resort to negative behaviour patterns when they feel frustrated or angry.

Toddlers are too young to understand what constitutes acceptable social behaviour and at their stage it is better to distract them when a difficult situation arises. Usually, by the age of four, a child has an adequate command of language and we can encourage positive social interaction. When Rory pushes Christopher because he wants the same toy, I acknowledge his negative feelings. I say something like 'I know that you are feeling angry because you want to play with that toy. But we aren't allowed to hurt other children. Christopher, tell Rory how you are feeling now'. Besides letting Rory know that his behaviour is not acceptable, I help him to verbalise his own feelings and to realise that Christopher has feelings too. It's okay to be angry, but it's not okay to hurt someone else when you're angry.

Children are still learning social skills. When a child is unable to cope with a situation, lead him away from it and allow him a 'cooling off' period. If necessary, provide something therapeutic, like crayoning or playdough, to help restore his equilibrium. Don't force an apology until he has had time to calm down – that would only teach him hypocrisy. Be ready to give a hug and offer moral support. After an opportunity for 'renewal', most children are quick to restore relationships.

Recently, in some 'comedy' video clippings on television, one character kept saying, 'I was so mad. I was so *mad* I just…' (followed by a tirade of what he had done in his anger). We seem to have gone from a generation which denied feelings, to one which uses feelings to excuse bad conduct. God's word doesn't say that our emotions justify our actions. 'If you become angry, do not let your anger lead you into sin…' (Eph 4:26). We all lose our cool and say things we shouldn't. But God gives us a chance to 'start over'. Let's reflect his love.

Discuss problems

By encouraging children to listen to each other, we can help them to respect others and solve their own problems. They learn to settle differences by talking about them. Discussion teaches children that other people have different viewpoints, and negotiation is a skill learnt through practice! In our family, when the children were younger, we used a large wooden spoon in family conferences. Only the person holding the spoon was allowed to speak. This encouraged us all to listen to each other without interrupting.

Offer choices

Very often children misbehave because they feel that decisions are being forced upon them. We all have different tastes and different moods, and we all like to do different things at different times. When we have the opportunity to choose we feel in control, and we will settle happily to a task if it's something we want to do. Offer the children an interesting variety of activities to keep them busy, and let them opt for something they enjoy.

If you provide a choice of activities at the start of the programme, the children will be more amenable to joining in the group time later on. Sometimes a choice of activity may be 'Do you want to pack up your toys by yourself, or do you want me to help you?' Even that option helps a child to feel he is involved and will lead to more co-operative behaviour. Life is about choices. Every minute of the day we are subconsciously making decisions.

> Children who have been given choices in early childhood will be more tolerant of one another because they recognise that there are alternative ways of doing things. As they progress in their educational life, they will be skilled in making decisions about what classes to take in higher grades, what kinds of friends to choose, how to dress, and all the other options that are available to youth today. They won't find it necessary to listen to everyone who claims to be a leader. Rather, because of their experience, they will be better able to discriminate between good leadership and bad; they will know better when to follow, when to choose an option and when to take the lead. *(Cherry)*

Discipline is not primarily about punishment. Rather, discipline is synonymous with guidance. If a child were able to express her needs, perhaps she would say something like this:

> Don't stride ahead of me – I may not be able to keep
>   up with you.
> Don't push me from behind – you may cause me to
>   stumble and trip.
> I ask you to walk alongside me,
> Gently guiding me through the difficult areas,

Pointing out the beauty of God's creation along the
    path,
Giving me the security of someone caring beside me
    all the way,
That your example may lead me
To understanding God's wonderful love for me.

Notes

1   Claire Cherry, *Please Don't Sit on the Kids*, Fearon Teacher
    Aids (US), 1983: I highly recommend this book, which pro-
    poses alternative discipline methods and provides practical
    'how to' steps to achieve them. Although the author is writ-
    ing from a secular standpoint, I believe that the type of per-
    son she perceives is a good model for Christian educators.

2   Gary and Ann Marie Ezzo, *Growing Kids God's Way*,
    Growing Families International Press (US), 1993.

Chapter 10

Helping the child to cope with loss

Today is a public holiday, and my husband and son have gone off on a hiking trail. I planned to use the day to work on this chapter. However, I am running behind schedule and battling to focus my thoughts which keep returning to two sad phone calls this morning from different sets of long-standing friends. Their grown-up daughters are both on the brink of divorce. It is so hard to know how to offer solace to grieving parents who are concerned that their children's marriages are 'on the rocks'. I can imagine the trauma of the daughters, each faced with having to make a decision that is going to have a far-reaching impact on her own life and the lives of others.

Sometimes, though, it seems that people in such situations are too wrapped up in their own pain to be aware of what others involved, especially any children, may be experiencing. Young children may not fully understand divorce procedures, but they still feel acutely the pain of losing someone they love. Today, when many people choose to live together without binding themselves to a marriage contract, a child's primary caregivers may drift in and out of a relationship without the harassment of divorce. But for a child, losing someone she has known and loved as 'Mum' or 'Dad' is painful, whether or not her caregivers are legally married.

Divorce figures are quoted as being about forty per cent in the UK, with some small variations elsewhere, so a significant proportion of children in any group will be affected. Sadly, even Christian marriages are no longer immune. Those who work with children need to realise that some of the children they are ministering to will probably be grieving for the loss of a parent-figure in their lives. This, of course, will sometimes be through death, and in thinking about what we *can* do to help children cope with loss we will first look at bereavement.

BEREAVEMENT

Death is the most final separation anyone can experience. The child under the age of two has no concept of it. He thinks that all objects are alive (animate).

Three-year-old Luke was visiting me while I was preparing visual aids for a song:

> Five red balloons are in the sky,
> Flying very high,
> And one red balloon went phh-phh-phhh,
> And four are left behind.

I coloured in five red balloons for the first line of the song. Then I drew a shrivelled little balloon. 'What's that?' I asked.

'The dead balloon,' Luke responded.

In his young imagination the five balloons dancing in the wind were 'alive', while the deflated one was no longer alive! It appears to the young child that things which move have life. Children often believe that their toys and pets think and feel as they do.

To children under four, death is a temporary state – they imagine that the dead person is in a state similar to sleep. Three-year-old Gretchen asks, 'When is Grandpa coming back?', even though she has been told that Grandpa is dead. She cannot grasp the concept that death is permanent and that the person will not return.

However, as children develop, so do their concepts, and they gradually begin to reach some understanding of death. They realise that some things – such as people and animals and plants – are alive; but others – such as stones – are inanimate. Four- to six-year-olds grow to understand that death is universal, that all creatures everywhere will die at some time. Even if parents have tried to shield them from this reality, children are inevitably exposed to death, perhaps through the media or perhaps through something like a pet dying. The burial of a deceased pet can, in fact, be an important part of the process of helping children come to terms with the concept of death. I'm sure we can all remember helping to dig the grave; wrapping up the body of some poor little hamster, dead bird or some other unfortunate creature; and then decorating the little grave with a cross and flowers.

By the age of six children begin to have a more realistic concept of death, particularly if they have experienced the death of someone they know. But even at this stage their understanding is limited. When four-year-old Tony's teacher tried to explain that his deceased aunt was now with Jesus, he asked, 'Why does Jesus like dead people?' Only when a child is more than ten years old does he begin to understand the concept of death more fully. 'Few children, unless they have experienced a long or severe illness, think of death in relation to themselves. To most children, death is associated with old people, and not with themselves' (Hurlock).[1]

Children will continue to have misconceptions about death if they don't have a caring adult to help them understand it. Be open to discussing death freely in simple, accurate terms, avoiding expressions like 'passed away' and 'called home', which will be confusing.

Children are affected not only by their exposure to death and the absence of the person who has died, but also by their observation of grieving adults. 'The child who is surrounded by gaunt-eyed adults who do not see you or hear a word that you say can magnify the idea of death's enormity almost beyond belief' (Barclay).[2] If death is viewed as an unbearable pain that cannot even be expressed, then children will probably come to fear it.

As children's carers, we can lend a sympathetic ear and offer practical help to grieving families. But perhaps our most important task is to be there to listen and give emotional support to the grieving child, who is often overlooked. Harold Bauman, in his booklet *Living Through Grief*, offers some advice on what to tell young children:[3]

> Only when we do not fear death ourselves can we communicate trust and confidence to our children. Our children can understand that God has prepared a home for those who love him. We do not say to a little daughter, 'God needed your mother more than you did,' or she may feel bitter toward God. Rather we say, 'Your mother is with God. And some day, when we come to die, we shall go to her.'

Just as children are no longer shut out from the mystery of birth, neither should they be shut out from the mystery of death. At this painful time they may feel a sense of abandonment, resentment or loneliness. To send them away to distant relatives or friends will only serve to increase these negative emotions. Rather, children need to be close to their immediate family and to experience the support, love and faith of those around them.

DIVORCE

I have heard it said that the problem with divorce is that the corpse is still walking around. Perhaps this blunt statement hits the nail on the head. The child who has lost a parent through death suffers the pain of loss, but the separation is final. For the child whose parents are no longer together, the loss is relived each time the child comes into contact with the parent who has left. Remarriage to another partner may be a disaster in his eyes, even if he likes the new member of the family. A child of divorced parents often harbours a secret wish that his parents will be reunited. Another marriage forces him to realise that this isn't going to happen. And the parent experiencing new feelings of love may not be sensitive to the child's grief.

Grief has been described as being like sliding into a pit. Various factors can cause us to begin the journey downward – not only death, but divorce, abuse, moving to a new home and

environment, or even the loss of a beloved pet – and those who are grieving may go through various identifiable phases. These are evident in children even though they may not be able to verbalise adequately what is happening. Let's look at each in turn.

Anger

Several years back, my husband required an emergency operation. Nobody said anything directly, but there was concern that he might have cancer. Thank God, the tumour was benign. However, for the first time I had to face my husband's mortality. The shock of possibly losing him caused an extreme and unexpected surge of anger which was, for some reason, directed at a very dear friend.

Fortunately, I had already trained as a LifeLine counsellor and gained some insight into the nature of grief. I recognised what was happening inside me and was able to deal with it without causing pain to my unsuspecting friend. I realised this anger was an expression of my grief. Yet, even though I knew it was illogical, I still had to work at coming to terms with the situation and with my own emotions. I wonder what hurt I might have caused if I hadn't understood what was happening and had been unable to stop myself lashing out.

If adults can react as I was tempted to, it is unsurprising that children, with limited reasoning and verbal skills, may express feelings of anger in a socially unacceptable way – through tantrums, verbal or even physical outbursts – possibly at those closest to them. Claude's father has recently walked out of the family home. Claude screams at his mother, 'I hate you!' Our response in such a situation might be to feel hurt or angry. Perhaps we would find it easier to cope if we understood that the child is battling with complex, negative emotions.

When a grieving child suddenly kicks the dog or smashes a treasured object, he may be trying to say something he cannot find words for. If he is experiencing frustration and anger, he needs to be handled with the same reassurance and care we would offer grieving adults. Punishing a child who is reacting negatively will only increase his rage. Rather, we need to guide him gently towards more socially acceptable outlets, and help him to find words for his feelings. For example, if a child has just thrown a toy across the room, an appropriate response might be 'I understand you're feeling angry, but if you throw the toy it may break. Let's find something else you would like to play with'. Acknowledge the child's feelings, gently letting him know that his action was inappropriate, and find him another activity, something that will help him 'let off steam' in an acceptable way. Activities that help hurting children vent their anger include playdough, puppets, a punch-bag, and a hammer, wood and nails. Just recently a newly divorced mother said to me, 'Your advice has helped. We're on our third punch-bag!'

Western society tends to discourage the outward expression of pain. A friend in the ministry, whose son died of leukaemia, shared with me that it took him a couple of years to work through his grief. It was only when he reached the stage of being able to tell God how mad he was with him that healing started to flow slowly into his wounded heart. We all need to be able to acknowledge (and own) our feelings. As child carers, we can lend support by having a listening ear and an empathetic touch. We all need a hug when the going gets tough, to know that someone cares and understands. Children's grief is very real, even though they may not understand it themselves. They have difficulty expressing their thoughts because their language is not yet adequately developed. They are still learning to put feelings into words. We can help by expressing what we imagine they are feeling, giving them the opportunity to 'own' their emotions and gently letting them know that it's okay to feel like that.

In a sense, we can act as a mirror. By listening sensitively and carefully choosing our responses, we can help the grieving child to 'see' himself in his situation and come to an understanding of his unhappiness. Recently three-year-old twins in my class were grieving the loss of their kitten, which they had seen savaged by their own dogs. Sarie came quietly to me and told me all about it, describing the gruesome event in detail and even drawing a picture of the kitten.

'So you're feeling very sad today,' I said gently.

She nodded, and we chatted some more about it. I assured her that her kitten wasn't hurting any more now and that Jesus was caring for it. (I don't believe that at such times it is necessary to debate theological issues concerning animals and the hereafter. If Jesus stated that the Father cared about every sparrow that fell, then I feel comfortable telling a child that God cares about her pets.) Interestingly, her twin sister hasn't mentioned the incident or indicated in her behaviour that she is upset about anything. Like adults, each child handles grief in her own way.

Bargaining

When faced with loss, many of us try to bargain: 'Oh, God, spare my partner, and I'll do anything you want me to!' or 'Oh God, save me now and I'll change'. Jane's parents are separating. She pleads, 'Come back, Daddy. I'll be a good girl.' Jane is concerned that it is her behaviour which has caused the rift, and tries to bargain to keep her family intact. A child needs to know that her parents' separation isn't her fault! Even if she doesn't overtly admit that this is what she feels, we can still gently reassure her that the break-up is her parents' problem, not a result of something she has done, and there is no need for her to feel guilty.

Denial

Some people go through a phase of denial – a recognised stage of grief, even for adults. Denial is not accepting the reality that the person is no longer with us. Children may fantasise about the missing parent, telling imaginary stories about going to the circus with Daddy or some other wistful dream. We must be very sensitive about how we handle this – they are not lying, only verbalising their hopes of their parents' reconciliation.

Depression

Depression is a strange and complex thing, at worst requiring medical assistance. Watch for changes in the behaviour of a grieving child, particularly if she becomes lethargic and withdrawn, or loses her appetite. If necessary, encourage her parents to seek medical help. Let the child know you care – even popping in for a visit can be greatly appreciated. It is recognised that grieving people need physical exercise, so encourage this too.

OFFERING SUPPORT

Whenever we suffer loss, whether through death or some other circumstance, we go through a period of mourning. Very often mourners say that the worst thing about their suffering is that nobody wants to talk about the deceased person. Often this is because we simply don't know what to say or are afraid that we will upset the grieving person. But we all need to express our grief, to remember the good times we enjoyed with the loved one. We need to remind ourselves that it's okay to cry: in fact, to cry brings healing, for men as well as women, for boys as well as girls. Be aware that a child may also need to talk about the loved person he is missing, and perhaps to cry.

Sometimes people who have suffered loss seem fine at the time – the symptoms of grief only become apparent a few days or even weeks later. Keep a careful eye on the grieving child in the period following his loss. I clearly remember twelve-year-old Joe standing tall and proud at his father's funeral, not shedding a single tear. Yet three weeks later I found him crumpled in a heap, his body heaving with tears as his loss suddenly hit him. I was so glad I was there for him when he needed someone: it would have been easy to have thought, 'He's coping fine.'

In South Africa our indigenous people have vastly different customs regarding the loss of a loved one to those of us from European backgrounds. The mourners grieve loudly during the funeral procedures, which generally take a full week and involve the entire local community. It is recognised that this kind of ritual actually helps the bereaved to deal far more effectively with their grief than Western traditions, where funeral services are often organised quickly and the mourners given sedatives to help them keep their composure. Their pain is consequently masked and often surfaces at a later date. I can't remember attending a funeral until I was in my mid-teens – my mother seems to have tried to shield us from death. But it's something children do need to be aware of, and they especially need to be given the opportunity to mourn if they have lost someone they care about.

ABUSE

This chapter would be incomplete without addressing the issue of child abuse. The loss of security, safety and one's sense of self-worth that comes through abuse, is possibly the most painful type of grief anyone can experience. The ever-increasing number of child-abuse cases, even within the so-called Christian home, is alarming.

When children are left in our care, we must ensure their personal safety at all times. The church has a responsibility to screen everyone who wants to work with children, even on a temporary, voluntary basis. In some countries this is a legal requirement, but even if it isn't, a church should have a written policy concerning the appointment and responsibilities of those involved in its children's ministry. It takes only a few minutes for an abuser to shatter a child's life! Don't bring anyone in without checking with reliable sources that they are people of integrity, and then monitor new volunteers carefully. If there is any doubt at all concerning someone's suitability as a child carer, the matter should be taken directly to the church leader or person in charge.

Recently I was aware of a youth pastor who invited a couple of pre-schoolers to come and see his office. Although I knew he was a man who could undoubtedly be trusted, I realised it was my responsibility to warn him that to invite young children into a secluded place wasn't good practice. Though I was confident this particular situation was safe, it would be natural for parents to be concerned if their children told them they had been alone with an unknown adult. To protect children and safeguard leaders' reputations, it is vital that churches ensure that every member has a clear understanding of their policy in children's ministry.

Circumstances in which abuse may occur

Marotz, Cross and Rush define neglect and abuse as 'any situation or environment in which a child is not considered safe because of inadequate protection that may expose the child to hazardous conditions or because of caretakers who mistreat or intentionally inflict injury on the child'.[4] Abusive adults come from all walks of life: abuse is perpetrated by professional people as well as by the poor and under-educated. Marotz *et al* state that for an abusive situation to arise, all three of the following factors are usually present at one time:

1   The characteristics of adults with potential for abuse/neglect. This description includes adults who were themselves abused as children, who have a poor self-image, and who believe that harsh physical punishment is necessary to discipline children. These people often suffer from drug- or alcohol-related problems.

2   The presence of a 'special child', eg one who is handicapped, disobedient or uncooperative, physically unattractive, unintelligent, hyperactive, fussy and/or clumsy, frequently ill, very timid or weak; the child may resemble someone that the adult dislikes.

3   Family and environmental stresses. Stress is often the 'last straw to break the camel's back' and may trigger the adult's abusive behaviour. This may be a major factor, such as divorce or financial pressures, or something as insignificant as a flat tyre or clogged sink.

Abuse may be physical, emotional or sexual. Marotz *et al* give the following descriptions.

Physical abuse

This is the easiest form of abuse to detect, as injury is usually evident. We may notice the following:

•   The child has repeated or unexplained injuries, eg burns, fractures, eye or head injuries.

- The child frequently complains of pain.

- The child wears clothing which may be inappropriate for weather conditions, to hide injuries.

- The child reports harsh treatment.

- The child is frequently late or absent, arrives too early or stays after dismissal from school.

- The child is usually fearful of adults, especially parents.

- The child appears malnourished or dehydrated, and chooses inappropriate food or drinks.

- The child avoids logical explanations of injuries.

- The child is withdrawn, anxious or uncommunicative – or outspoken and disruptive.

- The child is unable either to give or seek affection.

Emotional abuse
Unfortunately, this type of abuse is often difficult to detect and may only show its damaging effects later in life.

- The child is generally unhappy and seldom smiles or laughs.

- The child is aggressive and disruptive, or unusually shy and withdrawn.

- The child reacts without emotion to unpleasant statements and actions.

- The child displays behaviour that is unusually adult or childlike.

- The child has delayed growth and/or emotional and intellectual development.

Sexual abuse
Generally, twice as many girls than boys suffer from this form of abuse. It includes fondling, exhibitionism, rape, incest,

pornography and prostitution, regardless as to whether or not the child has consented. The signs which may be apparent are:

- Torn, stained or bloody underclothing.

- Complaints of pain or itching in the genital area.

- Venereal disease.

- The child has difficulty getting along with other children, eg she is withdrawn, baby-like, anxious.

- Rapid weight loss or gain.

- Sudden failure in school performance.

- Involvement in delinquency.

- The child is overly fascinated with body parts, and talks about sexual activities.

Remember that these are *possible* signs of an abused child: we should never jump to conclusions. One embarrassed mother came to me concerned that I would notice 'burn' marks on her son's back. Her older daughters had, in fun, given their little brother 'love-bites'! I knew the child had a loving, caring home, but it was a very good example of a case where wrong conclusions could have been drawn!

If you are concerned that some of the factors outlined above are present, observe the child over a period of time, keeping a dated record of all your observations. Be careful to write only what you actually see or the exact words used by the child. Don't note down what you 'think' may have happened. Date and keep any pieces of artwork that may be indicative of maltreatment. Abusive behaviour tends to follow a pattern which will become more evident over time as you carefully record it.

We have a responsibility to report cases of abuse to the authorities even if we are unable to prove our suspicions. They will always treat the matter in strict confidentiality, and are trained to give support and counselling.[5]

Notes

1   Elizabeth Hurlock, *Child Development*, 8th printing 1987, McGraw-Hill International Editions.

2   D Barclay, 'Questions of life and death', *The New York Times*, 15 July 1962.

3   Harold Bauman, *Living through Grief*, Struik Christian Books, 1991.

4   Marotz, Cross and Rush, *Health, Safety and Nutrition*, 3rd edition, Delmar Publishers, 1993.

5   A good resource for reference is *Safe to Grow: Guidelines on child protection for the local church and its youth leaders,* The Children's Working Group of the Baptist Union of Great Britain, 1994.

Chapter 11

The beginning again

We began with Dr Luke's observations. I would like to end by drawing together, out of subsequent chapters, the kinds of things we have discovered children need to develop – and which we need to help them develop now – in order to reach mental, physical, spiritual, social and emotional maturity,

A PERSONAL FAITH IN A LOVING GOD

A Christian friend once challenged me with the question, 'How do you know God loves you?' As I grappled with my answer, I came to realise that I know God's love through the love shown me by others. If I hadn't experienced love, I wouldn't be able to appreciate what love is. Children also learn through direct personal experience. We need to ask ourselves, 'Are other people experiencing God's love through their interaction with me?'

As young children's language skills are still incomplete, they are very sensitive to body language and will read a frown or a smile, folded arms or warm welcoming ones far more astutely than adults realise. Even an environment can affect children's perception of how they are regarded. Stand at the door of your meeting room and try to picture it from the viewpoint of a young child walking in for the very first time. Is it attractive and welcoming? Does it say, 'We want you to have fun here. We want you around'?

A BALANCED PERSONALITY

Children need to learn how to move their bodies and how to interact with others as much as they need to learn about the world around them. A balanced programme values physical, socio-emotional and spiritual development as much as cognitive development. In other words, it's not just a matter of sitting children down and filling their heads with Bible knowledge. They also require opportunities to participate in a way that will help them understand what the Bible is is saying.

It is universally recognised that children learn through play. Play is the natural way to ensure a child's total development. 'Play', however, doesn't mean leaving children to do as they please (though doing this from time to time will encourage their independence and creativity). Rather, we should be carefully planning stimulating programmes within which they can choose their activities. At school I noticed a small group of four-year-olds busy building towers with car tyres. As they played, I realised that this activity not only required physical skills (in lifting and balancing) but also social skills in the way they interacted with one another. As I have come to understand more about children's play, I have realised that this informal learning is far more valuable than sitting in a classroom 'listening to the teacher'. Children's play is children's work, and is vital for forming balanced personalities.

PROBLEM-SOLVING SKILLS

As the children in the playground hoisted the tyres one upon another, they were predicting what would happen as they added height to the tower. They were figuring out how to stabilise the structure by placing the larger tyres at the base to prevent it from toppling over. There was a sense of satisfaction as they achieved their goal: 'We can do things ourselves!' They were developing the ability to reason, and growing in confidence as a result.

An important aspect of problem-solving is realising that sometimes we make mistakes and we can learn through our

mistakes. The children learnt how to build a stable tower after repeated attempts that collapsed. As adults, we often want to 'do it for them', but if I had jumped up and said, 'Here, I'll build a tower for you', the children would actually have learnt very little. As educators, we can guide children's learning by asking carefully directed questions that will encourage them to analyse the situation and to seek solutions. We can help them create the situation in which they can proudly say, 'We *can* do it ourselves!'

RESPECT FOR OTHERS AND THE ENVIRONMENT

The children involved in creating the tower were learning to listen to one another, to share ideas and to give each other support. We learn to respect others when we ourselves are treated with respect. I mentioned earlier that I have a youngster in my nursery school who tends to resort to physical violence whenever anyone has a different viewpoint from him. It is part of my task to guide him into socially acceptable behaviour, and I'm helping him learn to communicate and to realise that others have feelings and ideas of their own.

'In everything do to others as you would have them do to you' (Matt 7:12, *New Revised Standard Version*). Children are more likely to follow our example when we treat them with respect, showing kindness and consideration, taking time to listen and trying to see things from their point of view. They learn acceptable social behaviour and how to handle their emotions through our affirmation as they play and interact together.

We can also help them to appreciate and care for their surroundings. Imaginative play – such as when children pretend to be Mummy or Daddy – is one way they can learn how to handle the world around them. And there are many other activities that naturally lend themselves to this, even small things like packing up after play. Children's natural curiosity makes it very easy to turn the smallest thing, such as an ant on a blade of grass, into a learning adventure!

GOOD COMMUNICATION SKILLS

Good social interaction is directly linked to the ability to communicate. Language is something we learn by doing, so we need to provide opportunities for this to happen naturally. Constructive play in small groups offers fertile ground for language development. And children may call us to share the excitement and wonder of a fluttering moth or raindrops trickling down the window pane. We may choose to let them savour the beauty of a moment in silence, or we may provide a 'running commentary' or start a discussion to help them gain the vocabulary they need to develop their knowledge. Like all good guides, judging when to be silent and when to speak requires sensitivity.

A POSITIVE SELF-IMAGE

Jesus said that we must love others as we love ourselves (Luke 10:27). In fact, we cannot truly love others unless we love ourselves. Loving oneself is respecting oneself and believing in oneself. It is being able to say 'I can!' As we help children learn to do things for themselves, we encourage their independence. The more they can cope with their everyday environment, the more competent they will feel. This ability to cope in life is what automatically helps us to feel good about ourselves.

Many small tasks, such as packing up, tying their own shoelaces and dressing themselves, build children's self-confidence. Our responsibility is to create a user-friendly environment for them to work in, and to teach them the skills they are ready to master – in other words, to help them do as much as they can for themselves and to provide safe, non-breakable equipment on which they are free to develop these skills. We can also help children take responsibility for their actions. For example, if a child pours his own juice and spills it, don't make a fuss. Just show him how to clean up and then encourage him to pour another drink. This will help him realise that it's okay to make a mistake (that's how we learn!) and that he can resolve the situation.

Doing things for themselves is one of the most powerful ways to build a positive self-image. In fact, creativity and problem-solving skills are directly linked to high self-esteem. The unsure person is afraid to take risks, yet it is only possible to find new solutions to situation when we are prepared to be risk-takers.

To recall the words of Luke, the wise physician, we are called to help the children in our care to grow wise and strong, to please God and to seek to be on good terms with other people. We have been given the opportunity to deeply enrich young lives. I can think of no higher calling!

OTHER RESOURCES FROM SCRIPTURE UNION

Sharing and Learning Together (The SALT Programme)
All-Age church resources

The SALT Programme (Sharing and Learning Together) is Scripture Union's pioneering teaching material for your church and children's groups, on Sundays or midweek.

SALT provides:

- Co-ordinated material for groups aged 3 to 13+ covered in four targeted age-bands, with additional material for adult and all-age worship.

- Exciting full-colour children's activity material for each group member.

- Menu-style choices which give leaders maximum flexbility in matching the needs of their group.

- A programme for the whole church family to share.

Leader's material	Children's material
(All quarterly A4 magazines)	
SALT: 3-4+	Sparklers (3-4+)
SALT: 5-7+	All Stars (5-7+)
SALT: 8-10+	Trailblazers (8-10+)
SALT: 11-13+	Lazer (11-13+)

SALT: All Ages

For FREE sample material for the SALT programme, write to:

SALT Samples, SU Sales and Promotions, 207-209 Queensway, Bletchley, Milton Keynes MK2 2EB. Tel 01908 856000; fax 01908 856111.

(UK customers only)

Everybody Praise: All-age Worship
A song book that encourages churches to promote a style and feel of worship which is open to children and families. Mainly new material, with some not-yet-easily-available songs, in a variety of styles.

Music book	**Words book**
1 85999 172 6, £13.99	1 85999 178 5, £1.99

Audio cassette	**Compact disc**
004 0, £8.99	005 7, £12.99

The ART of 3–11s
Age Range Tools for leading groups
Simon Marshall

Provides basic but essential practical help to leaders of 3 to 11s. Covers a wide range of subjects such as establishing the group's aims, developing effective ways of teaching the Bible, gaining confidence in planning a programme, discipline, pastoring children and relating to the rest of the church. Photocopiable pages.
1 85999 194 7, £7.00

How to Cheat at Visual Aids! Old Testament
Pauline Adams & Judith Merrell

A follow-on from the well-received *How to Cheat at Visual Aids* (see below), this volume deals specifically with Old Testament people, events and festivals. May be used with the original *How to Cheat...* or on its own. Photocopiable.
1 85999 161 0, £7.99

How to Cheat at Visual Aids!
Pauline Adams & Judith Merrell

People remember 30% of what they hear, but 60% of what they see and hear – that makes this guide to produing visual aids indispensable. Over 500 pictures of New Testament characters and stories. Photocopiable.
'...brilliant visuals for only a few pence each – time and time again!' *(Direction* magazine)
0 86201 990 7, £6.99

Pick 'n' Mix:
Over 100 ideas to create programmes for children of all ages!
Judith Merrell

An excellent resource for children's leaders (church, holiday clubs, assemblies, RE), *Pick 'n' Mix* contains ideas for icebreakers, ways of telling Bible stories, quizzes, crafts, games and creative prayers. Photocopiable.
1 85999 096 7, £6.99

Going Bananas!

Sue Clutterham

An action-packed programme for holiday clubs based on both Old and New Testament stories. Some Bible characters seem to have 'gone bananas for God, but these programmes show that loving, trusting and following Jesus is in fact the sanest thing anyone can do.

1 85999 097 5, **£6.50**

Also, see the **Going Bananas!** video:

Five Bible characters come to life before our eyes: Noah, Gideon, Elijah, Zaccheus and Jemimah (the woman with the jar of perfume).

1 85999 156 4, **£14.99**

These materials are available from Christian Bookshops, and from **Scripture Union Mail Order** (p&p extra) at:

PO Box 764, Oxford OX4 5FJ.
Tel 01865 716880, fax: 01865 715152.

All orders must be accompanied by the appropriate payment, including postage and packing as below:

Order Value	UK	Europe	Rest of World	
			Surface	Airmail
£6.00 & under	£1.25	£2.25	£2.25	£3.50
£6.01–14.99	£3.00	£3.50	£4.50	£6.00
£15.00–29.99	£4.00	£5.50	£7.50	£11.00
£30.00 & over	FREE	PRICE ON REQUEST		

Ask for a complete resources catalogue, free of charge.